T0343534

NO SECOND AMENDMENT, NO FIRST:

GOD, GUNS, AND THE GOVERNMENT

NO SECOND AMENDMENT, NO FIRST:

GOD, GUNS, AND THE GOVERNMENT

JOHN ZMIRAK

Published by

The Calamo Press
Washington D.C.

calamopress.com

Currente-Calamo LLC

2425 17th St NW, Washington D.C. 20009

© Copyright by John Zmirak

All rights reserved

Hardcover ISBN: 978-1-958682-04-3

Ebook ISBN: 978-1-958682-05-0

Printed in Canada

ACKNOWLEDGEMENTS

I would like to thank first of all Rev. James Robison and everyone at *The Stream*, where I have happily written for eight years, and where much of the writing here previously appeared in some form. (It is repurposed with *The Stream's* kind permission.) It has been an honor to work with these good people and pursue the same mission of fostering faith and freedom. Thanks to the indomitable editors of *Chronicles* Magazine for permitting the republication of an essay that appeared there. Thanks also to John Melton, former Executive Editor of *The Stream*, to Jason Jones, Eric Metaxas, Faye Ballard, and of course Finnegan and Rayne, without whom none of this would be possible.

To Jake Gardner, Ashli Babbitt, Rosanne Boyland, the prisoners imprisoned lawlessly after January 6, 2021, and all the other victims of Anarcho-Tyranny in America.

O Lord, save Thy people and bless Thine inheritance. Grant victory over their enemies to orthodox Christians, and protect Thy people by the power of Thy holy Cross.

TABLE OF CONTENTS

"I can no longer remain in today's Democratic Party that is now under the complete control of an elitist cabal of warmongers driven by cowardly wokeness, who divide us by racializing every issue and stoke anti-white racism, actively work to undermine our God-given freedoms, are hostile to people of faith and spirituality, demonize the police and protect criminals at the expense of law-abiding Americans, believe in open borders, weaponize the national security state to go after political opponents, and above all, dragging us ever closer to nuclear war."

–Tulsi Gabbard, former Vice-Chair
of the Democratic National Committee,
October 11, 2022

FOREWORD

By Eric Metaxas

I can never forget it. It happened in the early Eighties. Not long after I had arrived at Yale as a student, I was very solemnly advised by some new friends against having anything to do with a certain dark figure on campus who — I am obliged to tell you now, dear reader — eventually turned out to be none other than the author of the very book which you hold in your hands. Please don't be alarmed. I was quite a different person then, and the warning was dramatically misplaced.

By way of background, I was then nineteen or twenty, and as is generally the case with callow and feckless undergraduates, I didn't know what I believed, politically or theologically. So I had my finger in the wind, cravenly hoping thereby to move in the direction of whatever popular crowd might be willing to have me, and of course never dreaming that this method of travel might lead me toward — much less over — anything resembling an ideological cliff. I am almost sure that by that time I had not even ever heard the story of the Gadarene Swine.

And so it was during this period in my life that I happily fell into the company of a number of dedicatedly leftist humanities majors whose company I enjoyed, and from whom I carefully hid whatever traditional and conservative affinities I still harbored at that time, having grown up with working class

1

immigrant parents who had fled communism and *(shhh!)* loved America. At the time I ungratefully and naively assumed that — now that I had arrived at this august elite institution — I would learn what my parents didn't know and couldn't know, having never been to college. So I began to ape the views of my new "cool" friends on any number of subjects — such as whether President Reagan was a racist and fascist, or whether America was an oppressive colonialist power *(yes and yes!)*. The views of my new friends influenced me considerably, as I relate in my own book *Fish Out of Water: A Search for the Meaning of Life*.

I aspired to be just like these friends, whatever that meant, which is to say to bathe infrequently, to smoke cigarettes casually, to have no "puritanical" views on sexuality, and of course always and only to sport frayed and ill-fitting second-hand clothes from a local thrift shop. In short, I wished to cast away my genuine working-class roots for the faux working-class trumpery of those who had gone to boarding schools and were so wealthy that they must bend over backwards to run from it — and from Mummy and Daddy — in any way possible. So to wear something tailored or to have something cleaned, for example, would have been nothing less than sheer *hauteur*, not to say a loud slap in the face of all those less fortunate. Thus doth an ill-placed social conscience make cowardly slobs of us all.

So it was among these new Marxist/feminist friends that I learned of the dark figure who has all these years later written this book, and I well remember the moment. There were several of us standing together when one — let us call her Josefina! — grimly indicated to me a certain pasty figure then walking across the campus. But she did so with as much foreboding as if she had been pointing out one of those cursed figures from Hawthorne's fiction, as though he were a solitary, blighted figure marked by some secret sin, who moved about alone and rejected, wearing a mysterious black veil, and shunned by all those in acceptable circles. He was pointed out in a positively Shakespearean aside (cupped hand, hushed tones). I might have been debarking from a stagecoach in the Old West as the town's mayor's wife pointed out to me a scarlet woman lingering near the saloon.

It was one of those moments we've all seen a hundred times in films and TV programs, when someone morally judges another in no uncertain terms. And yet there was a *frisson* not merely of clucking judgement now, but of something like dread, too, as though this fearsome figure might have been Old Scratch himself casually roaming abroad in the weeds of an undergraduate. "D'you see that person?" my friend asked. I did, and averred as much. But who was he, whose very presence forced my friend to downshift to a hissing *sotto voce*? "That's John Zmirak," my interlocutor intoned. "He's a conservative Christian fascist." And these last three words were nearly spat out, as though even pronouncing them were an unpleasant but nonetheless vital duty, as though they were a trio of small toads that had somehow magically appeared in my friend's mouth, demanding instant egress.

And yet this foreboding wraith walking upright was about my height and looked quite unassuming and unthreatening. I couldn't imagine what it was he had said or done to provoke such horror. But of course, what did I know? And didn't I want to be on the right side of such issues? So I made a mental note of what I had been told and moved on. As it happened, I never had any particular dealings with this frightening figure. Although I now remember that he was in a literature course I took and seemed perfectly harmless. And yet I still cannot forget the palpable horror in the friend who warned me, as though she had pointed out a twenty-five-foot white shark making its way across a bay filled with swimmers and boaters, all tragically oblivious to the anthropophagous monster that glided so very menacingly near.

That long ago moment in gray, bleak New Haven is four decades ago, far in my past now as Pearl Harbor was from that moment. But I am from this present vantage point very happy to say — anywhere and to anyone, and more than ever to say here to you now — that that sinister figure against whom I was so ominously warned has become one of my dearest friends. Indeed, he is someone with whom I now cackle at least weekly as I interview him on my national radio program on any variety of issues. As Fred Willard's character asks in the mockumentary, *A Mighty Wind:* "Hey, wha' happen?!"

Actually, the answer to how I eventually came to see things from John's point of view — and no longer from those who warned me against him — is simple enough. After graduation I twisted in the wind, trying to be a writer, and eventually discovered that whatever advice and views my friends had imparted to me were insufficient in dealing with the world outside the coddled environs of an elite college, often known as "reality." I eventually became so miserable and so lost that in a moment of weakness I turned to the God of the Bible and almost instantly found the joy and hope and truth that I had been so sure didn't exist — that I had been told did not — and I came to realize that that moment of weakness was unquestionably the best moment of my whole life. My views on many things quickly began to change, and among these was my view toward the unborn.

Which is how — about twenty-five years ago in Manhattan, where my wife and I were attending a gala event raising funds for crisis pregnancy centers — I marveled to behold the very same John Zmirak who so chillingly had been pointed out to me all those years ago. Could it really be he? I fairly leapt toward him and quickly told him that I had known of him during our time at Yale, but had by now — rather obviously, given my attendance at this event — changed in my views of many things. I too was now serious about my Christian faith and deeply grateful for the country in which we were privileged to live. But I remember how much I wanted him to know how grateful I was to him for having held these views all the way back then — to have had the wisdom and courage and fortitude to hold them so heroically and so publicly, when nearly everyone, and myself at the top of that sad list, did not only *not* hold them, but demonized those who did.

So it is with something approaching that gratitude that I now warmly — but profoundly seriously and earnestly — recommend the book you have in your hands. Like most of what John Zmirak says and writes, it is entertaining and brilliant, but it is also extremely important. Which means that it is also extremely important that you do your part in telling others about it. Because it is in such acts of sharing the truth — especially when it might be difficult — that we pay back those who have done so before us, which of course we can never fully pay back. Nonetheless, let us try.

God bless you as you do.

Eric Metaxas
New York City
October 2022

INTRODUCTION

It's One Minute to Midnight

A book like this is a hard one to bring to a conclusion, if only because current events right up to the moment of printing keep vindicating the need for the arguments made here. As we were making final checks to the manuscript, a staggering abuse of power emerged by the governor of a U.S. state—directly linked to the central thesis here:

That American elites have adopted a dehumanizing, post-Christian view of the human person which undermines all our rights, especially our most basic right of self-defense against violence and tyranny recognized in the Second Amendment. The most effective practical tool these elites are using is a weaponized perversion of the concept of "public health." The vast abuses of individual liberties that were broadly accepted, even by many conservatives and church leaders, during the COVID panic set the precedent for the wholesale confiscation of our liberties, and with them, the guns our forefathers knew that we would need to protect them.

The latest outrage (another will likely have edged this one from the headlines by the time you're reading these words): The governor of New Mexico is using her executive power to strip some citizens in her state of their Second Amendment rights. She's not signing an unconstitutional law with the approval

7

of the legislature. No, she's issuing an order, and expecting law enforcement personnel to enforce it without question. She's hoping that politically sympathetic judges will wink at the obviously unconstitutional nature of her order, based on COVID precedents—and that if she gets away with doing this, that her actions will set a precedent for governors of other states.

As George Washington University constitutional scholar (and proud liberal Democrat) Prof. Jonathan Tooley wrote on September 9, 2023:

> New Mexico Governor Michelle Lujan Grisham on Friday suspended laws that allow open and concealed carry of firearms in Albuquerque for 30 days after declaring a public health emergency. The order, in my view, is flagrantly unconstitutional under existing Second Amendment precedent. It could also be a calculated effort to evade a ruling by making the period of suspension so short that it becomes moot before any final decision is reached by a court.

> Democratic leaders have increasingly turned to a claim used successfully during the pandemic in declaring a health emergency to maximize unilateral authority of governors. There have also been calls to declare racism a public health emergency, supported by groups like the American Public Health Associa-

tion. Transgender programs have also been declared a public health emergency by some groups. ... As the list of claimed health emergencies grow, even state Democratic judges may begin to balk at the obvious end run around constitutional rights.[1]

Mercifully, some local law enforcement balked, too. As the Post-Millennial reported:

On Friday, Bernalillo County, New Mexico, Sheriff John Allen announced that he has "reservations" regarding an order from Governor Michelle Lujan Grisham to suspend firearm laws for 30 days ... . "While I understand and appreciate the urgency, the temporary ban challenges the foundation of our Constitution, which I swore an oath to uphold" [Allen said].[2]

How political leaders like Grisham even contemplate unilaterally annulling constitutional rights? How are Americans tolerating such outrageous abuses of power? And why are our churches—at the time of our nation's founding the very hotbed of the fight for liberty—silent or even complicit? (The local Catholic archbishop, John Wester, came out in support of Grisham's order.) This book tries to answer those questions by drilling down to the core of the collapse of the Christian worldview in our country, without which (as our founders

NO SECOND AMENDMENT, NO FIRST

from Washington and Adams to Jefferson and Madison all said) ordered liberty is simply impossible.

You probably remember Kyle Rittenhouse. He was the seventeen-year-old who, in August 2020, went to Kenosha, Wisconsin, to defend property being destroyed during the violent anti-police riots dubbed by our media as "mostly peaceful protests." Rittenhouse shot three rioters who were attacking him, killing two. Prosecutors almost immediately charged him with homicide and attempted homicide.[3] Politicians, pundits, and the press called Rittenhouse a "vigilante" and a "white supremacist."[4]

But none of it was true. As should have been clear to any rational person—including the prosecutors—Rittenhouse acted in self-defense. He discharged a borrowed AR-15 style weapon responsibly and only as the last resort. Plenty of videos of the events emerged. From the raw footage, you can see a rioter chasing Rittenhouse into a parking lot and throwing something at him. You can see a mob chasing Rittenhouse down the street, sending him to the ground. You can see an assailant beating Rittenhouse with a skateboard and grabbing for his rifle. You can see another kicking him. You can see still another pulling a gun on the teenager and firing.[5]

A jury confirmed the obvious when it found Rittenhouse not guilty on all charges in November 2021. He was lucky that it wasn't a jury in Washington, D.C. or New York City.[6]

The media made a scapegoat of Kyle Rittenhouse even as we watched armed political gangs take over our cities. Blue-state mayors and governors let Antifa and its Marxist allies in Black Lives Matter (BLM) run rampant, causing billions of dollars in damage[7] in riots that killed at least twenty-five Americans[8] The media vilified Rittenhouse, simply because he was one of the few Americans to stand up and say "No." And prosecutors charged him with homicide even as thousands of arsonists and looters ran free.

Kyle Rittenhouse should never have been charged with a crime of any kind. He shouldn't have had to raise money for bail. He ought not to have had his name dragged through the mud. None of that would have happened in a country still connected to its founding principles.

But do you know what may be most remarkable about Kyle Rittenhouse's story? That the truth did ultimately come out. If you want a real gauge of the state of freedom in our country, consider the far lesser-known story of Omaha bar owner Jake Gardner.

Gardner used his own legal gun in an even more obvious instance of self-defense, which was also caught on video. But Gardner never got a fair trial, or a fair shake, from America. On May 30, 2020, he tried to save his elderly father and his own small business from the looting BLM mobs that were pillaging small businesses. Ann Coulter, one of the only journalists to report what really happened, wrote:

> During a BLM "peaceful protest" in Omaha, Nebraska, on May 30 (over George Floyd's dying of a heart attack while in police custody in Minneapolis), James Scurlock was peacefully protesting

by breaking into an architecture firm—hoisting an office chair and hurling it into two computer monitors, then ripping a phone from a desk and throwing it against the wall, as his friend shattered another monitor—all of which was captured on video.

Nearby, Jake Gardner, an Iraq War veteran and Trump supporter, was keeping watch over the two bars he owned, The Hive and The Gatsby, aided by his 68-year-old father and a security guard. The peaceful protesters soon made their way to Jake's bar, where they hurled a street sign through The Hive's plate-glass window. He and his father rushed outside to prevent the peaceful protesters from storming his bar.[9]

Everything that followed was caught on tape as well. One rioter charged at Gardner's father, sending him hurtling to the sidewalk. Gardner rushed over toward his father and urged the rioters to stop. He lifted his shirt to show he was armed. But a rioter assaulted Gardner from behind, knocking him to the ground, while a second hoodlum jumped on Jake too. Gardner fired two warning shots, sending his attackers away. But seconds later, a third assailant, James Scurlock, jumped on Gardner's back and put him in a chokehold. A desperate Gardner screamed, "Get off me! Get off me!" They wrestled and Scurlock reached for the gun. Finally, Gardner shot over his shoulder, hitting Scurlock in the collarbone. Scurlock later died from his injury.[10]

This was such an obvious case of self-defense that the county attorney, Don Kleine, declined to prosecute. Moreover, as Coulter notes, "At 22, Scurlock already had a rap sheet a mile long, including home invasion, assault and battery, domestic violence—and, of course, he was in the middle of a crime spree that very night. Methamphetamine and cocaine were found in his urine."[11]

But then the activists took over. A Democrat congressional candidate rushed to call Scurlock's death "cold-blooded murder."[12] Plenty of people smeared Gardner baselessly as a "white supremacist."[13] Local politicians, including Omaha's mayor, began pressuring Kleine. The county attorney caved. Although he insisted he wasn't "wavering in any way in the decision," Kleine agreed to ask a grand jury to review the case.[14] This time a special prosecutor, Frederick Franklin, would handle the case. Franklin, who is black, delivered the indictments that so many activists demanded. The grand jury indicted Gardner for manslaughter, among other charges. Don Kleine called a press conference to say that he hadn't seen any new evidence presented in Franklin's case and that he stood by his original decision not to press charges.[15]

That didn't matter, though. Gardner faced up to 95 years behind bars if he was convicted, thanks to prosecutors who had bowed to activists' demands to charge him.[16] He was widely condemned as a racist and a murderer. Even before the indictments came down, the owner of the building where Gardner had his two bars evicted him, forcing him to close down his family's business.[17] The landlord even issued an anguished statement to James Scurlock's family, extending his "deepest sympathy" for their "pain and suffering" and apologizing "for this horrible incident that happened near our building."[18] Gardner's supporters had set up a GoFundMe page to raise funds for his defense, but the Woke corporation shut it down.[19]

Jake Gardner saw no way out. Falsely accused, maliciously prosecuted, stripped of the right to counsel, this decorated U.S. Marine combat veteran took his own life. He could face down jihadists in Iraq but not Antifa thugs and politicized prosecutors in America.

There were no candlelight vigils for Jake Gardner. It's not as if he'd been a felon shot while menacing a cop. No murals depicted him as a Christ figure. No rioters chanted his name before looting liquor stores. In fact, a Nebraska Democrat state senator, Megan Hunt, went on Twitter to gloat about his death:

> The indictment of Jake Gardner would never have happened without the community, the people, who stood up for justice and demanded action from city officials. Jake Gardner is gone, but the white supremacist attitudes that emboldened him are still with us today.[20]

Our system broke Jake Gardner—and then, in a brutal irony, gave him a hero's grave in Arlington National Cemetery for his combat service abroad.

They Want to Hang All the Kulaks

Now, maybe you don't own a gun. Maybe you don't think Jake Gardner or Kyle Rittenhouse, or the right to keep and bear arms, has much to do with you.

I wrote this book to show you how much all these things matter—to you, to me, and to every other American—and how closely they're connected.

The image of human dignity that emerged from Judeo-Christian revelation and classical philosophy directly implies the right of self-defense and resistance to tyranny. In fact, the same human dignity that tells us not to tolerate slavery or racial segregation tells us that we must not let the state disarm citizens wholesale or leave the defense of their lives, liberty, and pursuit of happiness to the agents of a state with a monopoly on violence.

The right to self-defense must be zealously guarded. It protects the most fundamental right of all: the right to life. And it protects all our other rights and freedoms. Put it this way: If you have no Second Amendment, you have no First Amendment.

Of course, gun-control crusaders want you to believe the Second Amendment is a relic. They scoff at the idea that the right to keep and bear arms allows you to resist tyranny. President Joe Biden goes out of his way to mock that thinking. In 2022, for example, he said: "For those brave right-wing Americans who say [the Second Amendment is] all about keeping America independent and safe, if you want to fight against the country, you need an F-15. You need something a little more than a gun."[21] Biden has used that line (or something similar) a number of times.[22]

If the right to keep and bear arms is useless against tyranny, why have tyrants throughout history been so quick to disarm the people? Three legal scholars who did an in-depth study concluded: "The historical record shows that, almost without exception, genocide is preceded by a very careful government program that disarms the future victims. Genocide is almost never attempted against an armed population."[23] Similarly, law professor Nelson Lund says, "Governments bent on the oppression of their people almost always disarm the civilian population before undertaking more drastically oppressive measures."[24]

And yes, it still happens in the twenty-first century. Venezuela's dictatorial regime of Hugo Chavez and Nicolás Maduro banned the sale of guns and ammunition to civilians. The law, whose stated purpose was to "disarm all citizens," left Venezuelans defenseless. The state's forces killed nearly two hundred (unarmed) pro-democracy protesters in a year.[25] And remember the genocide in Darfur? Before that began, Sudan's Islamist regime disarmed non-Arab ethnic groups before liquidating them.[26]

In the twentieth century, the Nazis disarmed Jews and other political enemies at home, and they seized weapons in territories they occupied.[27] Communists disarmed the citizens before they even smashed the churches. Mao's Chinese Communists did it. So did Fidel Castro's Cuba and the Khmer Rouge in Cambodia.[28]

The Bolsheviks began disarming Russians almost as soon as they seized power. First only "the wealthy classes" would have to surrender their weapons,[29] but soon disarmament extended to "the entire population."[30] The Soviets stripped citizens of arms in every captive nation behind the Iron Curtain.[31]

How do you think the Soviets managed to send some twenty million people to the Gulag? If you doubt whether the right to self-defense protects your freedoms, read what the great dissident Aleksandr Solzhenitsyn wrote in *The Gulag Archipelago*, his account of his years in Soviet prison camps:

And how we burned in the camps later, thinking: What would things have been like if every Security operative, when he went out at night to make an arrest, had been uncertain whether he would return alive and had to say good-bye to his family? Or if, during periods of mass arrests, as for example in Leningrad, when they arrested a quarter of the entire city, people had not simply sat there in their lairs, paling with terror at every bang of the downstairs door and at every step on the staircase, but had understood they had nothing left to lose and had boldly set up in the downstairs hall an ambush of half a dozen people with axes, hammers, pokers, or whatever else was at hand? . . . The Organs would very quickly have suffered a shortage of officers and

transport and, notwithstanding all of Stalin's thirst,
the cursed machine would have ground to a halt!

If . . . if . . . We didn't love freedom enough.[32]

Do we love freedom enough? In the United States, we have
not lost our right to keep and bear arms—yet. But consider:
If a million Jake Gardners or Kyle Rittenhouses had stepped
forth in 2020, the riots would have stopped.

And the left is trying to take away this fundamental right.
They have gone to incredible lengths to try to criminalize gun
ownership in this country. When they can't get it done through
the legislative process (which is often), they use any means at
their disposal to prevent law-abiding Americans from exercising their constitutional right to keep and bear arms. They do
it by declaring as much territory as they can "gun-free zones."
They do it by getting lower-court judges to ignore both the
clear meaning of the Second Amendment and Supreme Court
precedent. (The Court upholds an originalist understanding of
"the right of the people to keep and bear arms shall not be
infringed.") They do it by suing gun makers and sellers into
oblivion. They do it by pressuring credit card companies and
sporting goods stores to create an illegal *de facto* registry of
firearms owners.

And they do it by scapegoating and destroying those who
use guns defensively, like Kyle Rittenhouse and Jake Gardner.
The most aggressive critics of self-defense present gun owners

not as citizens with rights but as depersonalized vectors of "gun violence" contagion.

As crucial as the right to self-defense is, the issues at stake extend further still. Apart from the indomitable Ms. Coulter, I'm one of the few people still writing about Jake Gardner. In fact, the thought of him haunts me. I think that God put him on my heart. Several times a week I remember that U.S. combat veteran and small business owner who was goaded to despair and suicide by Black Lives Marxists[33] and his own corrupted government.

Then I break down crying, as if we'd been friends.

And in a way, we have. I've met Jake Gardners throughout my life. Our country used to be full of them. Those weary-looking Greeks—refugees from a dictatorship—who ran all-night diners in Astoria, Queens, where I grew up, and bought nice two-family houses whose front yards they kept immaculate. Then on Greek Easter they'd dress up and march through the streets carrying lilies and candles and icons to their churches. They were Jake Gardners, too.

The sweet old Jewish couple whose cousins had all been murdered in "the Old Country," who ran the tiny Weber's Department Store under the El train and sold us the uniforms for our Catholic school. They kept a keen eye for shoplifters but were always kind to us kids. A Jake and a Jackie Gardner, absolutely. Or as they might have put it, they were *"mensches."*

The black and Korean and Latino business owners whose windows were smashed and property looted by mobs led by affluent Marxists slumming in somebody else's neighborhoods:

each of those storeowners was a Jake Gardner, too, in his or her way. I pray they've managed to piece back their livelihoods, and that the resentful layabouts who robbed them, unpunished, rot in prison for the *next* crimes they commit.

A Jake Gardner is an American who busts his hump, plays by the rules, keeps his word, breaks up fights, treats people fairly, fears God, distrusts the government, doesn't envy his neighbors, stands up for his rights, and defends the weak. He's not the sullen government worker who watches the clock and maxes out his sick days. He's the teacher who stays late to tutor troubled students. Or the weary mom who volunteers twenty hours a week at the crisis pregnancy center, helping teenage moms to keep their babies instead of killing them.

The Jake Gardners are what keep any decent country running. So if you want to wreck the place, they are the people you need to target. To cow, intimidate, break, and batter them into learned helplessness, so that the next time a violent mob charges down the street, they won't try to help their neighbors, as Kyle Rittenhouse did. They won't even try to protect their own dads, as Jake Gardner did. They'll let felons hopped up on drugs loot their businesses right in front of them. Jake Gardner wouldn't let that happen, which is why our homegrown Bolsheviks knew he must be destroyed. As a lesson to the others.

The founder of modern Marxism, Nikolai Lenin, had a word for the Jake Gardners of Russia. He called them "kulaks," and he hated them to the point of genocide. Here's what he wrote in an infamous telegram of August 11, 1918:

Comrades! The uprising by the five kulak *volosts* [regions] must be mercilessly suppressed. The interest of the entire revolution demands this, for we are now facing everywhere the "final decisive battle" with the kulaks. We need to set an example.

1. You need to hang (hang without fail, so that the people see) no fewer than 100 of the notorious kulaks: the rich and the bloodsuckers.
2. Publish their names.
3. Take all their grain from them.
4. Appoint the hostages—in accordance with yesterday's telegram.

This needs to be done in such a way that the people for hundreds of versts[34] around will see, tremble, know and shout: they are throttling and will throttle the bloodsucking kulaks.

Telegraph us concerning receipt and implementation.

Yours, Lenin.

P.S. Find tougher people.[35]

That's all you need to know about Marxism, right there—including its modern American versions, such as Critical Race Theory.

Those modern American strains of Marxism are no longer confined to fringe groups. They hold massive influence over elites in academia, the mainstream media, Big Tech, massive corporations beholden to "woke" ideology, and even our churches, which have increasingly surrendered to a post-Christian ethos.

By following this path, America's left has shown the foresight of the twentieth-century Italian Marxist Antonio Gramsci. From Mussolini's prisons, Gramsci observed that the Leninist formula of seizing power first, then transforming society ideologically, seemed destined to fail. He proposed instead that the left focus first on a campaign to influence, subvert, co-opt, and finally dominate society's non-governmental institutions. Political power would then fall into their hands like a ripe piece of fruit.[36]

Instead of being imposed from the top down, by the government, the new Berlin Wall is emerging from the ground up, with today's cultural Marxists building it brick by brick.

Don't believe me? Just think about the radical transformation of the American left over the past thirty years.

Imagine you went back in time to 1993. Do you think any of the people celebrating Bill Clinton's first inauguration—or even the conservatives opposed to Clinton—would believe you when you said that within a few decades the Left would:

- abandon "Safe, legal, and rare" for "Shout your abortion"?

- not only demand same-sex marriage as a basic human right but also persecute churches that don't approve of it?

- abandon their longtime skepticism of foreign wars, intelligence agencies, federal law enforcement, billion-dollar corporations, and censorship, and in fact wield their growing control over these institutions to silence their political opponents?

- deny the fundamental truth of biological sex and insist that there are more genders than flavors of ice cream, then demonize anyone who urges caution before giving children potentially irreversible hormone treatments or surgically mutilating them?

- condemn America's founding, embracing baseless conspiracy theories about our ancestors, despite the warnings of even liberal scholars?

- favor *de facto* open borders, the targeting as "domestic terrorists"[37] of parents who dissent at school board meetings, and the forcing of untested vaccines on millions of unwilling citizens?

- allow governors to place entire states under house arrest, with no legislative authority?

Nobody would have believed you if you said any of this. But it's exactly what has happened.

Now, as the Left has learned, political power remains difficult to hold onto. It's not quite the ripe fruit falling into their hands that Gramsci envisioned—though they may have felt that way upon the election of Barack Obama in 2008. The left greeted Obama's public appearances like the Jerusalem mob on Palm Sunday in *Jesus Christ, Superstar.* Early in the 2008 campaign, as Obama began attracting the adoring throngs, his wife admitted, "For the first time in my adult life, I am really proud of my country."[38]

Shortly before his election, Obama promised that he would go about "fundamentally transforming" America. And he embarked on that path as soon as he took office. During his two terms, his appointees politicized the FBI, the Department of Justice, and the Internal Revenue Service.[39] They took the vast, sweeping powers that Republicans had foolishly granted our intelligence agencies and weaponized them politically—as a few of us had warned was bound to happen.[40] The transformation he imposed on our country was supposed to be irreversible.

But then the American people stabbed their self-appointed leaders in the back on Election Night 2016. Virtually no one among the elites even considered that Donald Trump could be elected president. Trump's election felt like a cosmic betrayal, and leftists howled at the sky. Like far-right Germans in the 1920s, they descended into paranoia, hatred, and fantasies of revenge. Whole groups of citizens now became domestic "enemies" or stooges of foreign powers ("Russian collusion").

The Left now treats anyone who disagrees with them— anyone, that is, who defends beliefs that prominent progressives held just a few years ago—as evil, dangerous, and worthy of personal and professional destruction.

Abandoning Our Ancestors

Although the Left could not hold political power eternally, its zealots still wield enormous influence throughout our culture because they dominate our most important institutions. And they have indeed transformed our country. As a result, we have turned away from certain truths on which the United States was founded. The Founders fought our War of Independence, created our system of government, and drafted our Constitution based on those truths. These items in our national creed appear both explicitly and implicitly in their debates and public writing. State constitutions, public sermons, private letters, and other records also inscribe the views about man, his rights, and his nature that our Founders held in common.

Our Republic was premised on the eternal truthfulness of certain assertions about the human person. Our legal system rests on them, and the stunning prosperity, stability, and freedom we have enjoyed in subsequent centuries go a long way toward proving that our Founders' beliefs were right.

But the current generation isn't learning those truths—not in our schools or even in our churches. From our law schools and court opinions, to our media and teachers colleges and seminaries, Christian humanism and moderate Enlightenment views about the proper role of government have been ousted by newer, less humane ideas. Progressivism, which views human beings as more akin to social insects than sons of God, has long prevailed among our elites. Cultural Marxism, which views all social relationships through a jaundiced eye, has tainted our view of our forefathers. Shallow utilitarianism, which seeks to pile up happy moments for ignorant consumers, has replaced the Christian vision of man as a dignified but fallen creature made in God's image to live in ordered liberty.

Our system of government wasn't designed with these radical new ideas in mind, and it won't function properly if its laws and principles are systematically reinterpreted to match them. But we see this reinterpretation happening all around us. Judges distort the plain text of the Constitution. Lawyers offer false and crass arguments that betray our basic principles, and these arguments prevail in court. Unelected, unfireable bureaucrats seek to wield vast powers incompatible with our freedoms, and lawmakers empower them to do so.

The heritage we received from our ancestors is increasingly endangered. Unless we awaken to the problem, what's genuinely exceptional about the American system will fade into history, and the world will lose its last best hope.

This book is a modest attempt at restoration, at reweaving the ancient tapestry of truths that made our Republic possible and carried it through many crises up to the present. Consider it an act of grateful patriotism by the grandson of immigrants from an embattled, desacralized Europe.

Part I of this book explores the degeneration of the Judeo-Christian worldview that made possible the founding of a self-governing, free republic such as the United States of America. It shows how supernatural faith gave way to wistful "spirituality," and a firm grasp of the natural law (that set of moral truths knowable by reason alone) as the basis for making just laws for free individuals surrendered to humanitarian tinkering by an ever-more powerful state. Instead of citizens created in the image of God, afflicted by the Fall but offered Redemption, responsible for their actions, we now see ourselves and our neighbors as termites in a hive—dependent on top-down management and constant protection by our "betters." These elites in politics, media, academia, and multinational companies arrogate to themselves a superhuman status. They plan for the "future of the planet" based on partial, politicized, dogmatic theories that they exempt from rational scrutiny and enforce via censorship, "canceling," and even direct financial penalties inflicted on dissenters. In this section, the right to keep and bear arms serves as the test case, the prime example, of how our political masters are confiscating our rights in the name of protecting us from ourselves.

Part II provides a roadmap for rolling back this dehumanizing movement and training ourselves in sounder modes of reasoning about politics and theology, which accord with our own traditions and beliefs. Here, the right to armed self-defense again is used as an example of sound and unsound reasoning, of authentic reflection on man's nature and the proper limits of government, as opposed to inhuman and anti-human modern ideologies.

Part III offers a detailed historical study of the crucial political question at the center of this book: how the biblical view of man helped create (unique to the West) a philosophy of freedom, which rejected rigid hierarchies and other tyrannical

NO SECOND AMENDMENT, NO FIRST

structures. How is it that a country such as the United States of America came about, predicated on the idea that man has such an intrinsic moral dignity that he must not be subject to governments that violate his rights? Where did our Founders get the idea of building into the Constitution they were drafting a mechanism such as the Second Amendment, which keeps the people armed so that they can serve as the final bulwark against tyranny? What are the biblical, philosophical, and historical roots of American ordered liberty, and how can we preserve those roots against those who are even now attempting to hack down the tree?

Any patriotic citizen should wish to know the answers to those questions, and how he can help pass on to his children the same sacred heritage he received from his ancestors.

PART I

HOW THE BIBLICAL WORLDVIEW GAVE WAY TO A PROGRESSIVE HIVE MIND

CHAPTER 1

MASS SHOOTINGS, MASS DELUSIONS, AND THE PANIC ATTACK OF OUR CHURCHES

Sadly, as you read this, it is all too likely there was recently a mass shooting in the headlines. That tragic fact says a great deal about contemporary America, from the alarming rise in untreated mental illness to the precipitous decline in respect for the institutions of church and family that for so long were the moral foundation of our communal life.

But needless to say, in the media reports on the shooting, there will have been no such thoughtful reflection, any more than there will have been professions of gratitude if the intended victims were lucky enough to be in a place where it was legal to defend themselves, and they were therefore able to take down the perpetrator with minimal harm to the innocent.

No, we know perfectly well how the stories in the mainstream media will have read, and what liberal politicians will have said; and, unless you've been very blessed or very discerning, even how your own church will have responded to the event. Why? Because journalists, leftist flaks, and massively funded anti-gun activists might as well have a template on their computers, so interchangeable do the statements seem whenever a mass shooting occurs. You can say the same for bishops, priests, and ministers. They have only to plug in a few simple facts, dates, and names, and Presto! Before the blood of innocent murder victims is even dry on the pavement, their document is finished. The statements are ready to be posted in news stories, editorials, social media posts, and parish newsletters, quoted by lazy reporters, highlighted in tweets, and touted in speeches to Congress.

The fact that these statements are almost impossible to tell apart from one another won't blunt their impact. Quite the contrary. The very prefab quality of this Astroturf replacement for grassroots public opinion is one of its strengths. If you don't look closely, the monotonous sameness can resemble a consensus. An "awakening of common sense" in the face of "an epidemic of gun violence." The blaring of the unified message from every mainstream medium won't get dismissed as propaganda but cited as a groundswell. Millions of joiners will mistake the Kool-Aid they imbibed for their own considered conclusions. They'll bleat "Four legs good, too legs baa-aad!" as eagerly as the sheep in George Orwell's *Animal Farm*.

And their shepherds won't waste time learning the actual details of the crime. They'll pause, of course, to see if they can find a racial, ethnic, or other Woke angle to exploit. Was the shooter a "primary oppressor"? (That's the term for "straight white male Christian" used in Intersectional Theory, which rules academia and has infiltrated our seminaries.) If so, then they'll have a cudgel to use.

But what happens when a mass shooting turns out not to be the work of a "primary oppressor"? What if it's some angry Syrian immigrant, or deranged jobless crack addict, or a BLM enthusiast? Often anti-gun activists, including reporters, can't even be bothered to wait. On March 24, 2021, a shooter claimed ten lives in Boulder, Colorado.[41] While police were still sitting on details, Twitter was awash in noise about "white supremacy," "toxic whiteness," and "Christian nationalism." Some of those tweets would soon be deleted, but others would linger (facts be damned!), because wasn't racism still a problem? Sure, this mass shooter was a Syrian refugee of the kind Barack Obama recruited, and whom Donald Trump was a racist for wanting to send elsewhere. But at base weren't mass shootings, no matter who commits them, *all* part of a toxic white male "gun culture"? That culture is the real enemy, not the shooters.

Have no fear, little ones. The elites who stir up ethnic hatred of white people and sexual hatred of men won't be deterred. Give them a day or so to tweak their press releases, and you'll hear them bleat as usual about how the slaughter of Americans teaches us that . . . Americans must be forcibly disarmed by their own government.

Then we'll be safe.

Weaponizing "Public Health"

There'll come the renewed demands for background checks (which already exist), for bans on a variety of guns unlike the one the shooter used, for outlawing accessories that law-abiding hunters and target shooters find helpful, like silencers or scopes. The calls will come for more "gun-free" zones, even if the shooting occurred in such a free-fire zone, where citizens walk defenseless. However many gun laws the shooter violated—not being, apparently, the law-abiding type—we'll find ourselves barraged with demands for more laws. Honest citizens will obey those laws. Mass shooters and ordinary criminals will flout them.

Most of all, we'll be treated to dehumanizing and fiercely un-American rhetoric, expressing the shallow worldviews of elite opinion and its enforcers. These are the views embraced by the professors at our most prestigious universities and the teachers who train our young people. And arguably even worse, these are the beliefs of the pastors at every level of the churches of too many denominations.

The fact is, the stance that the Left takes on the right to keep and bear arms reveals a coherent anthropology, a view of human nature. It's just one that stands *directly opposed to the traditional, American, and biblical worldview.*

This new picture of man is complex and deeply depressing, and it's the source of countless micromanaging, secularizing policies unrelated to guns but that likewise threaten our freedom, demean and demoralize us, and help to fill our prisons, abortion clinics, and marijuana dispensaries . . . and empty our churches. Even so, professional churchmen are some of the loudest voices asserting it.

In fact, orthodox Christians and defenders of the Second Amendment have a great deal in common. And it's not just that they're often the same people. Nor that distinct members of each group might back the same political candidates or face common opponents in today's America. Nor even in the demonstrable fact that the right of self-defense and resistance to tyranny enshrined in the Second Amendment has its roots in the particular histories of the English people, the Protestant churches, and America's earliest settlers.

It goes even deeper than that. It lies in the profound shared conviction of human dignity that emerged from Biblical revelation and classical philosophy.

After long, grinding months of medical tyranny, when state governors refused to lift bans on even outdoor religious gatherings and dragged out the virus-driven lockdown of our economy, it's more important than ever to insist on the basic liberties guaranteed by our Constitution. It's especially important now that mobs led by Marxist organizations spouting revolutionary slogans have toppled statues of U.S. Founders, abolitionists, Union generals, and Catholic saints, and threatened to smash "white" images of Jesus. Angry, lawless crowds took over whole districts of cities, with police ordered to stand down.

Except, of course, when citizens step up to defend themselves and their neighbors. Those people, like Kyle Rittenhouse and Jake Gardner, got the full attention of police and prosecutors.

When the governor of New Jersey can go on national television and admit that he "wasn't thinking about the Bill of Rights" when he outlawed religious services,[42] America clearly needs a wake-up call to defend its founding principles. When the mayor of New York City can threaten to "permanently close" places of worship if they flout his quarantine orders,[43] we have entered dangerous territory. When governors arbitrarily deem gun shops and church services "inessential" but abortion clinics "essential,"[44] decreeing which businesses must close and which may open, we're ripe—indeed *overdue*—for a reassertion of fundamental principles.

Among its many other destructive impacts, the COVID crisis greatly empowered activists who would weaponize "public health" to erase constitutionally guaranteed, God-given rights of American citizens. And those activists have targeted the right to keep and bear arms, which is enshrined in the Second Amendment. Crusaders for gun bans have long claimed to work in the name of "public safety." More and more, you'll hear them talk about guns and "public health." In fact, in 2021, the director of the Centers for Disease Control and Prevention (CDC) declared that "gun violence" posed a "serious public health risk."[45] The legacy media and other allies have dutifully embraced the language. NPR, for example, ran a story headlined "What it would take to treat gun violence as a public health crisis."[46]

Emboldened, President Joe Biden has called for a ban on the most popular civilian rifle in America, the AR-15,[47] and he has spoken scornfully of the Second Amendment's primary purpose—as a backstop against tyranny.[48] Although the Supreme Court has gradually moved toward a more originalist understanding of the Second Amendment, the balance on the Court could easily change. The growing divide between committed churchgoers and America's traditional gun culture could weaken support for self-defense in party platforms and future legislation.

How Our Sold-Out Churches Dehumanize Us All

The moment is now to insist on the deep religious roots of our rights as individuals and upon the theological, biblical, and historical case for the traditional American philosophy of government, based on liberty constrained by natural law.

Rather than talk in abstractions, let's read the actual statements of leading church groups in the wake of mass shootings to see how far such groups have drifted from traditional Christian morality and into politicized virtue signaling. For the sake of completeness, I'll cite post-shooting statements of churches across the denominational spectrum.

The National Council of Churches is the umbrella group that speaks for such mainline Protestant religious congregations as the Episcopal Church, the Presbyterian Church USA, and the United Church of Christ. In 2019, after a mass shooting, the National Council of Churches issued a statement that read in part:

> We are deeply discouraged by the awareness of the near certainty that our elected officials will not respond in any meaningful way to this violence, for they are collectively and shamefully within the captivity of the gun lobby. Our elected leaders are guilty of negligence and cowardice.

> Incendiary language from leaders also must be boldly and consistently condemned and countered. Racist, inflammatory rhetoric must be replaced by words and deeds that create beloved communities, ones that embrace ethnic, racial, and religious diversity. These are the values we wish to see in a vibrant, inclusive America.

> The combination of readily available weapons of mass destruction and a toxic white racist nationalist ideology is a recipe for disaster. If we cannot confront these two evils, far greater violence and social disruption awaits our nation.[49]

Apart from the long list of Woke buzzwords that these religious leaders incant, what's the most notable thing in this statement? The use of bloodless, impersonal, public-health jargon to describe horrific acts by mentally disturbed or evil individuals aimed at other individual citizens. These churchmen can't speak of "murder." They don't cite the Ten Commandments. They say nothing of the sanctity of life or even the rights of the victims. Instead, they speak of guns as if they are evil totems in a fetishistic religion, and they talk of "gun violence" as if it were a newly emergent virus or an atmospheric pollutant. When they do engage moral issues, it is only to chide politicians and the "gun lobby" for resisting specific legal measures to restrict Americans' constitutional rights. The statement nowhere acknowledges those rights—the rights of citizens to defend themselves from threats.

Here the relevant moral agent is the state. The bearer of rights is not the person made in the image of God but the nebulous "community" or society. A more relentlessly collectivist way of framing political issues would be hard to find outside Venezuela or North Korea—except in some public health agency discussing another proposed COVID lockdown or vaccine passport scheme, likewise without concern for the rights of mere citizens.

Mainline Protestants aren't alone in taking this approach. In the wake of religious Modernism's sweep through Catholic institutions in the 1960s, U.S. Catholic bishops now advocate progressive policies on every hot-button issue from entitlement programs to immigration. Today, with the exception of a few issues on which past Church teachings at infallible levels of authority tie their hands (abortion, and some questions of sexual ethics), the bishops have transformed themselves, collectively, in the image of the National Council of Churches.

Here is the official statement the U.S. Council of Catholic Bishops released after a mass shooting in 2019:

> We can never again believe that mass shootings are an isolated exception. They are an epidemic against life that we must, in justice, face. God's mercy and wisdom compel us to move toward preventative action. We encourage all Catholics to increased prayer and sacrifice for healing and the end of these shootings.
>
> We encourage Catholics to pray and raise their voices for needed changes to our national policy and national culture as well. We call on all relevant committees of the United States Conference of Catholic Bishops to outline a reinvigorated policy agenda and pastoral campaign to address ways we can help fight this social disease that has infected our nation.
>
> The Conference has long advocated for responsible gun laws and increased resources for addressing the root causes of violence. We also call upon the

President and Congress to set aside political interests and find ways to better protect innocent life.[50]

Cardinal Blaise Cupich, whom Pope Francis appointed as Archbishop of Chicago, offered the most blatant example of moral aphasia after pro-life undercover journalists exposed Planned Parenthood's profiteering in the harvested organs of aborted babies in 2015.[51] In an op-ed in the *Chicago Tribune*, Cupich stunningly found a way to equate this vile, inhuman practice with Americans' defense of their Second Amendment rights (among other leftist hobbyhorses). He wrote:

> While commerce in the remains of defenseless children is particularly repulsive, we should be no less appalled by the indifference toward the thousands of people who die daily for lack of decent medical care; who are denied rights by a broken immigration system and by racism; who suffer in hunger, joblessness and want; who pay the price of violence in gun-saturated neighborhoods; or who are executed by the state in the name of justice.[52]

Nor are Evangelical Christians immune to this powerful trend among the churches. Strong cultural pressures to avoid losing young believers, escape media caricatures, and curry favor with elites increasingly influence Evangelical pastors and churches.

In 2019, the *New Yorker* ran that rare thing in its pages, a glowing portrait of an Evangelical Christian organization.[53] The subject was the pressure group Heeding God's Call to End Gun Violence. Youthful, idealistic, and poorly catechized Evangelicals—along with those who crave respect from elite publications—are drawn to organizations like this one. In its public statements on gun issues, Heeding is virtually indistinguishable from mainline Protestant and post–Vatican II Catholic organizations. The following comes from one of its press releases issued after a mass shooting:

> To us at Heeding the logical direction to start is to focus on the weapons that made killing and injuring so many in El Paso and Dayton so very easy, as they have in so many other places in the country. We call to "Demand the Ban," namely a prohibition on manufacture, sales, transfers and possession of military-style semi-automatic assault guns.

> We understand there are many issues at play regarding this weekend's violence—white supremacism, racism, immigration and many more and we stand in solidarity with all those seeking to solve them. However, it has always been Heeding's way to focus our attention on one issue at a time and,

for many reasons, we focus now on Demand the Ban, because there is no legitimate reason to allow citizens to possess these killing machines. We doubt not that God, by whatever name, is with us and that our work is truly worship.[54]

The talking points here are familiar. So are the weaponized buzzwords. More crucial is the worldview slippage that the statement signals. These Evangelicals have wandered away from concern for individual rights and personal responsibilities. They've lost interest in—if they have not already abandoned—traditional doctrinal positions. They no longer use the natural law reasoning that ought to unite believers around the law "written on the human heart" and knowable by reason. Instead of sins that need God's forgiveness or virtues that we sinners must cultivate, we face "plagues," "epidemics," "syndromes," and "social structures" that will yield only to government action, provoked by political activists.

What would a more solidly grounded Christian response to the monstrous evil of a mass shooting look like? Not finding one readily available, I decided to craft one. Please contrast it to the post-Christian, Woke texts you just suffered through. It's a statement that virtually any Protestant or Catholic pastor could release, or deliver from the pulpit, in the wake of the next outrageous attack on innocent life using guns.

A Sermon in a Season of Violence

Dearly beloved. Today we gather to pray together, to obey the words of Jesus, who asked us to share bread and wine "in remembrance of me." In one of the paradoxes of our faith, such gatherings are bloodless reenactments of his redeeming death on the cross. In the midst of life, we remember death. Gathering as we do in the hope of life but under the shadow of death, we can take some comfort that we Christians are more prepared than the pagans to face moments of darkness, horror, and sin.

The people who fell last week were our neighbors, perhaps our friends or even family. Besides being fellow souls walking with us through this vale of tears, the men, women, and children whom the killer targeted were our fellow citizens. People joined with us in the very special, particular bond that is America. Like us, they looked to a government of ordered liberty to protect their inalienable rights. For that purpose our forefathers formed these United States of America. If you read the words of the men of faith who designed our nation, you will see that almost to a man these preachers and pastors saw in America something unique, fragile, and special.

They saw in these far-flung colonies of a city on hill, a place where the people and not some prince, the citizenry and not some conspiracy of the powerful, would wield the levers of government. A place where the solemn power of the state would be wielded in the light, not in the shadows of court intrigue or bureaucratic lethargy. The light of which I speak is cast by a very particular source. It shines from the face of every human being, made in the image of God and redeemed by his very own Son.

In a dark and prophetic novel, *1984*, George Orwell had the spokesman for a modern, godless tyranny describe a future in which the will to power would reign unchecked and citizens would be reduced to cringing, manipulated slaves. "If you want a picture of the future, imagine a boot stamping on a human face—for ever," he wrote. Orwell had seen the rise of the Nazi and Fascist regimes, which created vast industrialized mechanisms of genocide. He watched the misguided dream of socialism turn into the sprawling slave state of the Soviet Union, with its labor camps and murder squads. He feared that the whole world might succumb to one brand or another of totalitarianism. And he depicted that grim possible future with an attack on the human face.

One of the most ancient Christian devotions entailed meditating on images of Jesus's wounded face. Too many pastors this weekend will be offering sermons that lose sight of that face. Too many of our leaders will react to outrageous crimes like the one our community suffered, but forget the human face—the faces of the victims, individual citizens with dignity, value, and inalienable rights. They'll forget the face of the killer, a man who is either deranged or wicked. They won't speak of the outrageous, sickening sin that man committed. They won't remember the rights of each of the victims he assaulted. Instead, they will speak in broad, vague generalities about the "problem" of "gun violence," as if inanimate objects were jumping out of stores and killing people. As if the tools we Americans use for hunting, sports, or self-defense were viruses, which we must address as a public health crisis, with bans, confiscations, and basic rights stripped away.

The modern temptation is great to avoid talk of sin and forgiveness, of good and evil, of the rights of the human person and those who threaten them. Instead, we are taught to should think of the enormous, nebulous "community," whose well-being we measure in aggregated statistics.

Today both Mammon and Caesar would have us forget the face of Christ and our neighbor. They want us to see our country as more like a termite colony, or an anthill. In such collectivist species, the person is replaceable, perfectly interchangeable, and the only fate that matters is that of the hive.

America's Christian Founders saw the deadly danger in such political systems. They feared the rule of tyrants and the rise of demagogues. They refused to worship Caesar, and, like the early Christians, they put their lives on the line for their convictions.

In the media, we rarely see the faces or hear the stories of the victims of mass killings like this one. For a few days, some will morbidly dwell on the scattered thoughts and hateful writings of the killer. (Unless the killer is a "transgender" avenger, targeting a Christian church, as happened in Nashville in 2023 —then the manifesto will be kept secret by the police.) After that, the drumbeat of groupthink that fills our opinion pages, and too many of our sermons, will return to its default mode: collectivist tinkering. The reporters and TV commentators, the legislators and ministers, won't ask what fatherless homes, or untreated mental illnesses, might lay behind a crime like this one. Nor will they ask why the victims were helpless to save themselves in the "gun-free" zone that the legislature created, which too often really means a "free-fire" zone, as citizens crouch helplessly behind couches or desks, waiting for the faraway police to at last arrive. No one on TV will talk about that outrage.

No one will ask why these Americans were forbidden on pain of jail time to exercise a basic constitutional right to defend themselves, a right as fundamental as freedom of speech or the exercise of religion.

Instead, we'll hear from the usual well-funded suspects about the latest scheme to render more citizens helpless with calls to "cure" the "plague" of "gun violence." When someone insane or evil, or equal measures of both, attacks our fellow citizens and strips them of their rights, it's simply not Christian to step back from their faces, forget their identities as persons, and instead think of ways to strip even more of our fellow citizens of even more of their rights.

It's also un-American.

Today as we pray for the victims and their families, and for the conversion of the criminal who inflicted this evil, we must recommit ourselves to cherishing, protecting, even safeguarding the rights of every American, including the most basic right it's even possible to imagine: the right, in the moment of danger, to defend himself and his family.

Amen.

FROM THE IMAGE OF
GOD TO A SAD SACK

Doesn't that sermon seem as if it came from another century or planet? That's no accident, or quirk of literary style. The mindset of our elites, including most of our churchmen, has shifted overwhelmingly away from classical moral categories and Christian moral premises. The fear of Hell and hunger for Heaven have given way to wistful hopes of Utopia right here on earth, right now—or at least in the wake of a raft of "social reforms."

Instead of an image of God who wields the fearful power of free will that shapes his eternal destiny, the human person became . . . a sad sack, a grab bag of dysfunctions, more to be pitied than censured. Conversely, if we don't respect his free will enough to condemn his sins, we won't feel obliged to respect the individual rights that our Constitution guarantees him. We will come to see both moral judgment and individual rights as archaic holdovers from a world before addiction counseling, social science, and rehab. And that is how Christians turn into great big squishy trash bags full of vague "Woke" compassion but empty of principles, unwilling to take risks or sacrifice to help their actual neighbors, and ready to shed one guaranteed constitutional right after another, if that's the price of a peaceful, mediocre life.

CHAPTER 2

FROM THERAPEUTIC MORALITY TO ANARCHO-TYRANNY

I f you were to massively alter an animal's DNA, would you expect it to survive? What if you spliced alien genetic material into its brain? At the very least, you'd expect a huge change in the creature's nature. Well, that's exactly what many Christian churches have done: excised the most basic moral principles that have guided them for millennia and grafted in alien, incompatible elements.

And the outcome is as you'd expect: the judgments, policies, language, and pastoral attitudes coming out of these churches are fundamentally altered, too. They constitute a whole and entirely different "new gospel"—precisely the kind against which St. Paul warned.

Let's take my own Catholic Church, since I know it the best. One of the finest Catholic philosophers out there is John Gravino. He has written a compelling book called *Confronting the Pope of Suspicion*.[55] In it, he argues that Pope Francis's agenda is to rewrite the foundations of Christian morality. Francis does this via his writings and the people he appoints to positions of power. The result? An Astroturf upsurge in demands for our church to bless same-sex unions, among other post-Christian perversities.

Of course, Francis isn't some lonely revolutionary. What he's doing began in the early 1960s in Catholic circles, and much earlier than that in mainline Protestant denominations. It's creeping into Evangelical churches even as you read this.

How did it happen? Cowed by the prestige of "Science" and gaslit into believing Freud's tenuously evidenced (and now largely discredited) theories which fell under that rubric, Catholic leaders in the early 1960s discarded one worldview for another. Instead of the biblical picture of man as free, fallen, and responsible, theologians and teachers embraced Freud's view that, rather than crippled by sin, then redeemed by Christ, we're afflicted by "repression," then liberated by a therapist.

To the new way of thinking, insisting on Biblical morals was no better than clinging to 1950s-era segregation. Sexuality isn't a gift from God to be used within his intentions. It's a primal, overwhelming force, like the lava from a volcano. Attempts to control it are dangerous, damaging, and futile.

And advocating Christian ethics amounts to hate speech aimed at sexual victim-groups.

Gravino shows how critical textbooks used for training priests shed all talk of sin and forgiveness for discourses on "self-fulfillment" and "actualization."[56] He documents how this radical shift in emphasis was closely followed by catastrophe. Not just the collapse in numbers of vocations for priests, brothers, and nuns, but something infinitely worse: the clerical sex abuse crisis.

The very seminaries where this new "liberating" worldview was being taught produced hundreds of priests who would go on to "explore" and "actualize" their sexual impulses with . . . underage boys. Those same schools also formed bishops who would send offenders for a few weeks of therapy, then reassign them to parishes or boys' schools full of fresh new victims. When the scandal about all this exploded, they switched straight back to repression. Not of sexuality, of course, but of the facts of what they'd done.[57]

The Therapeutic Roots of Tyranny

The shift from a morals-based culture to a therapeutic one can corrupt the state as well, as we've seen since the advent of COVID, with millions willing to throw away their liberties with both hands in a desperate concern for "public health." This mass surrender, however, is merely the last stage in the process of trading our freedoms for promised safety.

This shift was an inevitable consequence of those changes occurring in the churches. It can be seen, for instance, in society's increasingly liberal attitudes toward criminality. The social scientists analyzing the problem have now ruled out the Christian worldview of sin and forgiveness.[58]

This change in attitude was gradual and, so we thought, enlightened. Moving from simply punishing youthful offenders to understanding the social dysfunctions that had produced them was the right and moral thing to do. After all, we were a modern, civilized society. Our scientists could split the atom and put men in space. Surely we could crack the code of what sent young people astray.[59]

Those who imbibed Freud's fundamental ethics made it *verboten* to blame easy divorce or illegitimate childbearing for burgeoning social chaos. Didn't Alfred Kinsey's studies of sexuality offer reams of (falsified) data to back up Freud's point? Their totem of easing repression created its own taboo: traditional Christian teaching. Christian morality no longer stood as an ancient, time-tested source of wisdom. Rather, it came to be seen as "rigid" and "suffocating"—indeed, as the *cause* of societal dysfunction rather than the solution. Its answers, by definition, were illegitimate.

Suddenly everyone from the academics at your local college, to your therapist, to the "experts" in the popular magazines you read were casting doubts about the idea that adultery was immoral, suggesting that this belief was "medieval," the equivalent in ethics of six-day, "young earth" Creationism in paleontology.[60]

As long ago as the 1950s, Stephen Sondheim had gently mocked the emerging post-Christian therapeutic attitude to morality in *West Side Story's* classic song "Gee, Officer Krupke," wherein teenage hoodlums mockingly embrace the emerging post-moral view of criminal justice:

Dear, dear, dear kindly Sergea Krupke you gotta understand
It's just our bringin' up-ke that gets us out of hand
Our mothers all are junkies, our fathers all are drunks
Golly Moses, naturally we're punks.[61]

There's a flip side to all this, of course. The witty teens who wield the mushy rhetoric of the therapeutic state also understand they can have it both ways. Should they actually get arrested, they'd expect lawyers to appear on their behalf, and they'd want those lawyers to present them not as cynical hoodlums but as victims and to cite and defend their legal and civil rights.

Those rights—stable, legally enforceable claims against the power of the state—didn't arise from the murky, dehumanizing theories of psychologists and sociologists. They emerged many centuries before, the fruit of the biblical worldview, which sees human beings as essentially free, responsible agents made in the image of God.

In this worldview, the reason we must be held responsible for crimes is that the abuses one commits harm other free human beings, who, as creatures of the same God, likewise bear the stamp of dignity. The rights these teens would have hoped their attorneys insist on emerged from centuries of struggle between the people and the government, from Anglo-Saxon customs, canon law, Norman common law, and contests between English parliaments and power-hungry kings.

Legal rights most of us still treasure, such as the presumption of innocence, trial by jury, and the adversarial system of justice (i.e., you get a defense attorney), are all implied by the older, Christian view of the person. But none of these old-fashioned concepts fits in with the new, therapeutic model. If we can transfer people's responsibilities (such as their guilt) onto "society," we can likewise transfer their rights. We can choose which people or groups to tar with collective guilt for "systemic racism" and punish or disadvantage through affirmative action, and which ones get carte blanche for street violence and political intimidation—as Democrat governors and mayors chose not to prosecute thousands of rioters in 2020, then savagely prosecuted even the most peaceful January 6 protestors, seeking and getting decade-long sentences for misdemeanor crimes.[62]

Treating People Like Viruses

As with so many aspects of the new, post-Christian worldview, this dehumanizing tendency emerges most clearly on the topic of gun rights. We no longer think in terms of individuals, their rights and wrongs, of holding each soul responsible for the choices he makes before God. Instead, we view masses of people in the aggregate, the way a factory farmer might make calculations about his pigs. We seek to "minimize violence" statistically, by calculating what factors might most easily be changed in some equation, to yield a better average behavioral outcome among interchangeable featherless bipeds. Just as ruthless pet owners have been known to declaw their cats, or even surgically "de-bark" their dogs, unprincipled politicians grasp at easy answers to complex questions of crime and social pathology. They decide that the most obvious solution to violence is to declaw and de-bark all the citizens. Once you have abandoned the premise that individual human beings were created by God on purpose, each with an eternal destiny, you won't feel the sting when you strip them of fundamental human rights, such as the right to defend themselves and their families from violence, or to rebel (if finally necessary) against a tyrannical government.

"Red Flag" laws are an apparently innocuous but profoundly insidious example of this temptation in action. Politicians of both parties tout such laws, also known as Extreme Risk Protection Orders (ERPOs), as a sane, "moderate" response to the "gun violence epidemic." The laws even sound plausible at first. In essence, they empower a judge to take away someone's guns based on the testimony of a credible source that this individual poses a threat to himself or others. Supposedly, they take from likely offenders the means of violence and thereby save innocent lives.

In truth, they represent a radical attack on the most basic principles of Anglo-American jurisprudence.

Under Red Flag laws, the burden of proof is not on the government or your accuser. It's on you, the gun owner. You don't get a free lawyer, as criminal defendants do. You must pay to fight this seizure of your property. The person who lodged a false accusation? He can sit back and relax. The state does his job for him, and he faces no effective penalty for lying.

Writing for *The Federalist*, Dana Loesch summed up the problem with such laws:

> The people who report your Twitter account and your Facebook pages because they dislike your opinion want you to trust a government-run system where people can, without serious penalty of law, report you and have your property confiscated before you're allowed to defend yourself in court weeks, even months, later.[63]

Quite simply, Red Flag laws let any hostile neighbor, ex-wife or husband, or one-time yard contractor who resents bad Yelp reviews pick up the phone and make a "safety" complaint about a gun owner.

The police pass it on to a judge. He reads the accused citizen's emails and social media posts. He has to decide whether he wants to risk leaving guns in this citizen's hands. There is no downside for the judge (who quite possibly agrees with most of his colleagues that the Second Amendment is crazy) in seizing these guns. But on the 0.0000001% chance that he doesn't take the guns and this citizen does shoot someone? That judge's career is devastated. What do you think his default decision is likely to be?

The police then can show up without a search warrant, or even a warning, to seize all the citizen's guns.[64] And the burden of proof, from here on out, is on the citizen to hire a lawyer and prove to a judge that he isn't a dangerous extremist or future school shooter.[65] Keep in mind that gun grabbers in various states have adduced "a strong interest in guns" as evidence that someone is dangerous. So the very fact that you want to own any guns is an argument you shouldn't have them. No due process allowed.

The Bill of Rights Is a Buzzkill

The Bill of Rights is a buzzkill. In fact, the whole Constitution is. Or that's how you see those documents if your main interest is power. If you think you're vastly better than your fellow citizens, much wiser and purer and saner than the "Deplorable" masses, those antique institutions are irritating speed bumps. As French economist Frédéric Bastiat warned us, lovers of big government and social engineering see themselves as talented gardeners and the rest of us as hedges.[66] It's the job of the coastal elites, their captive media and universities, and the federal government to prune us and shape us like topiaries into pleasing shapes.

Which Americans are threatened? Those who belong to any of the following groups:

- Populist conservatives whose leftist neighbors resent them.
- Home schoolers whose conformist neighbors think they are "weirdos."
- Christians or other conservatives who speak up at school board or children's library meetings against X-rated sex education or drag queen story hours.
- Anyone with a vengeful ex-lover or spouse.
- Employers who fired somebody once.

With Red Flag laws, the gun grabbers, who want Americans to turn into disarmed, passive subjects of coastal elites, will have almost everything they want. Unable to pass laws banning guns wholesale, they'll outsource the job to lefties (or simply the "Karens") in the population at large.

What if, for the sake of fitting in and not offending anyone, we decided to sign on to all of this? To agree that "Safety first!" is the key takeaway from the Gospel? Then why shouldn't we continue our outreach to progressives by extending that principle to plug *all* the dangerous holes in the Constitution?

That was precisely the point Justice Samuel Alito made in his decision in *McDonald v. Chicago*—that the nips and tucks people are so ready to make to the Second Amendment could easily get applied to all the other liberties in the Constitution.[67]

Alito noted: "The right to keep and bear arms ... is not the only constitutional right that has controversial public safety implications. All of the constitutional provisions that impose restrictions on law enforcement and on the prosecution of crimes fall into the same category." Make loopholes for the government to violate one such right, and you've set the precedent for vitiating any of them, should those in power find it convenient.

Our elites come for the Second Amendment first, but why should they stop there? Why should they put up with the whole array of constitutional freedoms based on the traditional, Christian view of man as responsible, dignified, and free? They seem convinced they know better than their fellow citizens who, according to Barack Obama, "cling to their guns or religion." The ignorance of such backward people makes them threats to both social justice and public health. Eliminating the old "freedoms" is the right and moral choice, then.

How interesting that the term born in leftist circles for their spiritual superiority was "Woke." That's the antonym of "asleep." Let's take their metaphor seriously. If you believe that almost half the country are stumbling somnambulists, unconscious or in denial of the world's fundamental truths, do you really trust them with the same rights as you? If you believe that superstition, racism, ignorance, groundless conspiracy theories, or simple hatred motivate your fellow citizens, how likely are you to compromise with them? To respect their freedoms? To treat them as adults with equal rights?

Human nature being what it is, you're far more likely to keep them from power "by any means necessary" (to quote Malcolm X). For their own good, and everyone else's. You'll accept dishonest legal decisions that empty the Constitution of meaning. You'll support destructive attacks on people's character, whether it's "Covington Kid" Nick Sandmann (with whom NBC, CNN, and the *Washington Post* settled defamation lawsuits)[68] or Supreme Court justice Brett Kavanaugh. You'll demonize and caricature your opponents and their motives. You'll endorse elaborate conspiracy theories yourself, like the Russia Collusion hoax—and shrug without any shame when they are exposed as baseless.[69]

Our New System of Government: Anarcho-Tyranny

In blue cities and states—many of the most populous places in America—the right to bear arms has been more trampled on than any other fundamental freedom guaranteed as God-given and sacred in the Bill of Rights.

Or has it?

Consider the phenomenon of "cancel culture." Think about how narrow, constrained, and defensive our speech has become online. Because social media are not officially part of the government, the Left tells us all the time that as "private companies" (many of which are effective monopolies) they need not hew to constitutional standards. They can censor, edit, prescribe, and ban with all the vigor of an old-fashioned publisher—all the while hiding behind the legal fig leaf that they're "neutral platforms," as Congress deemed these companies in Section 230 of the 1996 Communications Decency Act.[70]

It is the most laughable fiction in public life today—which is saying something.

How exactly is a social media company neutral when it bans the account of a U.S. president, embraces official orthodoxy on fighting a virus while banning alternative views, and dictates that Christian doctrines amount to hate speech or verbal "violence"?[71]

Airlines collude to maintain "no-fly" lists of citizens under no legal conviction for terrorism. [72]

Credit card and online payment companies collude to forbid donations to groups with disfavored political views.[73]

Private citizens whose political donations get leaked can lose their jobs.[74]

In fact, we can see in the behavior of many Democratic politicians the outlines of a new practical doctrine of politics. The only term that could do it justice is "anarcho-tyranny." Each of those words, "anarchy" and "tyranny," represents one extreme on the spectrum of government power over the citizen. So, at first blush, the name of this political doctrine suggests self-contradictory nonsense. Anarchists oppose the very existence of government. Tyrants are rulers who expand their power relentlessly, in defiance of national customs and natural law. What would it even mean to say that someone favors both anarchy and tyranny?

In theory, the purpose of government is to maintain order and promote justice among vast numbers of people. The human dignity of other sovereign human beings is a firm barrier to our grabbing everything we want and hoarding it in our basement, or putting our neighbors into drab matching uniforms and forcing them to do patriotic gymnastics. We must learn to tolerate other people's "absurd" beliefs and distasteful choices in return for their putting up with ours. We rely on good manners and common decency most of the time to blunt the clashes among us, and only when those civil habits fail us must we turn to the cops and the lawyers, and the threat of fines and prison.

Our country's Founders called such an arrangement "ordered liberty." Think of it as Aristotle's "Golden Mean," or the sweet spot between "Somali warlords fighting over who gets to steal your farm" and "North Korean soldiers staring coldly at you through the barbed wire."

But for Americans today neither total anarchy nor absolute tyranny is the real danger. The real danger is rather a creative amalgam of both, in which the government doesn't do the short list of things it's supposed to but steps right up and takes over a long list of tasks it has no business trying. A nation ruled by such a hybrid system:

- Leaves its borders wide open to human traffickers, even as it stations troops in dozens of other countries.
- Uses the state to grind down the basic institutions of civil society on which its own democracy was built,

while spending billions to try founding democracies in the Muslim world. Or fix the outcome of border disputes between corrupt Slavic oligarchies like Russia and Ukraine.

- Restricts political speech aimed at influencing elections and legislation but allows pornography to wash over its young people, even in public school curricula and libraries.

- Permits and even funds the killing of innocent unborn children but refuses to execute murderers and terrorists.

- Meddles in the child-rearing choices of well-ordered married couples but lavishly subsidizes teenage pregnancy.

- Admits hundreds of thousands of refugees who belong to a religion incompatible with the nation's constitution and culture while rejecting those with the tolerant faith of its founding.

- Helps overthrow foreign regimes that repress that hostile religion and puts into power extremist movements that wish to impose it everywhere by force.

- Batters and recklessly redefines the most basic institution of society, marriage, and makes the legal covenant on which it's based completely unenforceable through no-fault divorce.

- Lets politically like-minded rioters torch and loot entire cities, as police are ordered to stand down, but aggressively prosecutes citizens who dare to use force in self-defense, much as pro-Nazi mayors in Germany in the 1930s let Brownshirt thugs off with wrist-slaps, while imprisoning anti-Nazis who resisted them.

Today's anarcho-tyrant realizes that the very existence of churches and families stands in the way of his own exercise of power. They are barriers against the complete domination of the state, the media, and the educational establishment, and these are his chosen instruments of social control.

So he argues that the free expression of traditional religious beliefs and family values oppresses those he designates as "victims" (including, for instance, pornographers, professional abortionists—and their customers). In his view, traditional beliefs retard the process by which absolute "equality" of those who flout those beliefs is to be achieved and result in their "stigmatization" and "exclusion."

Old-fashioned liberals would once have accepted religious exercise, if reluctantly, as the price of liberty. But the anarcho-tyrant has progressed far beyond such eighteenth-century scruples. Wielding the claim of "liberating" oppressed minorities, he will use the power of the state to repress the speech and actions of millions—the *majority*—of private citizens.

Of course, once a tipping point is reached—once the "oppressed" groups, such as the LGBT movement, become more powerful than their "oppressors"—logically the liberation movement should be over. But the anarcho-tyrant knows better than to dismiss his most fervent soldiers till the war is completely won. He will demand, *is* demanding, unconditional surrender of traditionalist forces. He will not be satisfied until every church preaches, and every local school teaches, the same "liberating" creed—which is to say, until they have been effectively annexed by the state. That is what has happened with the "patriotic" Catholic Church in China. The church has freely rewritten the text of the New Testament, the better to suit "Chinese cultural characteristics" and the power of China's Communist Party. This even extends to mutilating inspired sacred scripture. Arielle Del Turco of the Family Research Council explains how a textbook for a government-run university translates the Bible's book of John, chapter eight:

In this passage, an adulterous woman is brought to Jesus, and her accusers ask if she should be killed by stoning for her sins.

In every authentically translated version of scripture, Jesus responds, "Let him who is without sin among you be the first to throw a stone at her." These words disperse the angry crowd, and Jesus tells the woman, "Go, and from now on sin no more" (ESV).

The Chinese Communist Party's version takes a different turn. In this telling, the crowd leaves, but Jesus tells the woman, "I too am a sinner. But if the law could only be executed by men without blemish, the law would be dead." Then Jesus proceeds to stone the woman.[75]

Increasingly, the Left acts like the religious police of an angry theocracy. And why shouldn't it, when for millions the Woke movement has taken on both the function and the authority of a traditional religion, but without the core elements of reason or revelation that might constrain its use of power?

Progressive Christianity, with its soft and squishy therapeutic nostrums, has progressed right past the words and intentions of Christ and become a "new gospel." It has usurped the power of traditional churches of the past, even as it mimics their structure.[76] It offers pseudo-religious enthusiasm to the lost, especially in universities and among the young.

We have entered a Great Awokening, a vast wave of irrational moralism. The Woke cult is a pathological development of basically Christian impulses, but as wholly unhinged from their proper function within the Body of Christ as a tumorous organ might be inside our abdomen. And in each case, that cancer kills.

CHAPTER 3

FROM THE SOCIAL GOSPEL TO THE NANNY STATE AND BEYOND

Since churches have been colonized by adherents of statist paternalism, especially among their elites, Second Amendment advocates face a challenge in making their case to many Christians. This paternalism historically has its roots in the "Social Gospel" movement of the late nineteenth century. Geological discoveries revealing how old the earth really is, and Darwin's speculative attempt to explain away the apparent "design" in animals and man, raised doubts about the reliability of the Bible on historical and doctrinal questions (i.e., the special creation of mankind, the existence of Adam and Eve, and hence the fact of Original Sin requiring redemption by Jesus Christ). After brief attempts to contest the implications of such theories, many churches we now identify as "mainline Protestant" surrendered. They began to shift their emphasis away from personal holiness and evangelism.

Christianity could no longer be trusted, these clergymen claimed, to tell us *how things are.* That is the domain of science, they said. Of course, a role still existed for men like themselves, and progressive theology faculties and churches, they hastened to add! Christianity remained the source for *how things ought to be*: how we should treat the poor, for how we should organize politics and reform both the economy and the law. They presented Christianity more as an elevated philosophy of man, intended to preserve his traditional dignity from the ancient fossil beds into which Darwinism threatened to ditch it. Jesus became an exemplar, an inspiration, a "great moral teacher"—albeit one who tended to insist on his own divinity and perform public miracles, culminating at last in his resurrection from the dead and ascension into heaven.

That is, if we trust the text of the New Testament. But modern biblical critics were ready to help with that. For centuries, political intellectuals from Machiavelli to Hobbes had aided monarchs eager to aggrandize the state at the church's expense by finding "creative" new ways to explain away the plain sense of the Bible.[77] In the Enlightenment, thinkers eager to secularize the culture applied these skills to the texts of the Bible, attacking not just the traditional Christian readings applied to them but even the texts' authenticity and reliability. Especially in nineteenth-century Germany, in the legally established churches of the Second Reich, state-funded scholars produced an entire methodology which they called the "Higher Criticism."

While it entailed a wide array of apparently "scientific" techniques, at its core this mode of Bible reading was dedicated to eliminating as "inauthentic" any trace of the supernatural. Hence, every miracle attributed to Jesus had to be seen as a later "interpolation," added on by a "church community" instead of attested to by eyewitnesses. Scholars strained every nerve to date the texts of the four Gospels themselves as late as possible, sometimes well into the second century—the better to render them essentially legends, with a mysterious man at their center, whose ethics we find appealing.

Although some churches (the Roman Catholics, and among the Protestants, the Fundamentalists) for decades resisted this movement to denature Jesus' morals from his manhood and Godhood, those with the most social prestige in America largely embraced it. They gradually ceded ground on doctrinal questions, while insisting that Christian ethics of kindness, "social justice," and concern for the poor remained untouched by doubts about biblical inerrancy, the Fall of Man, or even the miracles of the New Testament, culminating in the Resurrection of Jesus.[78]

Kneeling Before Caesar Instead of Jesus

How to make Christian ethical concerns effective, given churches' own fading belief in eternal punishment or reward?

By implementing them through the state. Churches that adopted the "Social Gospel" became virtual hatcheries for political activists of the dawning Progressive movement, which saw either full-on socialism or an omnicompetent welfare state as the means by which the "Kingdom of God" could be made real on earth in our own time and by strictly human (governmental) means.[79]

Instead of individuals submitting themselves to the will of God and voluntarily taking part in the traditional "works of mercy" commended by the Gospel, citizens would be "educated" in public schools, "organized" by the central state, and compelled by law to sacrifice their own autonomy, wealth, and liberty for the "common good."

The most extreme example of the "Social Gospel" becoming political was the presidency of Woodrow Wilson. President Wilson saw his administration, and especially his engineered U.S. intervention in World War I, as the hand of God at work in history. He decisively reoriented the Christian mission in Progressive terms to refer to social change accomplished by the state.[80] That Social Gospel thumper and arch-Progressive, himself the son of a Presbyterian pastor, seemed to believe that the Holy Spirit had put him in the White House. And he regarded political power in his own righteous hands as the straightforward instrument of Divine Providence. Lance Morrow writes:

At one point during the Paris Peace Conference, [Wilson] seemed to suggest that he was actually an

improvement on the messiah. Lloyd George listened
in amazement as Wilson observed that organized
religion had yet to devise practical solutions to the
problems of the world. Christ had articulated the
ideal, Wilson said, but he had offered no instruc-
tions on how to attain it. "That is the reason why
I am proposing a practical scheme to carry out his
aims."[81]

The Holy Spirit, Wilson apparently believed, wanted
him to make the Gospel real by imposing social justice, global
peace, and eugenic experiments. The power to make these
improvements would come from bayonets, bullets, and prison
cells. Even before he became a presidential candidate, Wilson
was writing tomes about the need to sweep away the dusty
obstacles to real (i.e., virtually absolute) presidential power.[82]

Once in office, Wilson virtually extinguished free political
speech in America, imprisoning opponents and critics of U.S.
involvement in the war[83], among many other constitutionally
questionable measures. He transformed the income tax—sold
to Americans as a tiny levy on multimillionaires—into a large-
scale means for redistributing wealth. More importantly, that
wealth and power left private hands and fell into the hands of
the state. Over next the century, the federal government would
replace civil society (individuals, churches, free civic organizations) as the primary movers of day-to-day American life. We
began to look more and more like the Prussian-run German
Empire we'd just defeated in World War I.

Once the state replaces the church as the locus of man's salvation, what room is left for the older, Anglo-American Protestant ideal of the individual as bearer of sovereign rights, including the right to defend himself, his family, his liberty, and his belongings from direct assault by criminals, or tyrannical governments? Almost none at all.

A century and a half after the rise of "Progressive Christianity," we can see the outcome in the positions taken by mainline Protestant churches on a long list of political issues, from economic to regulatory. Instead of trying to aid individual souls in deepening their relationship with God, these institutions have become little more than incense-perfumed Non-Governmental Organizations, offering theological support to projects of completely secular origin, aimed at furthering a vision of the "common good" far removed from Christian values.

This is why so many of these progressive churches are silent if not outright pro-choice on the sanctity of unborn life, and why they readily jettison other traditional Christian moral positions on sexual ethics. Rather than prophetic witnesses to an otherworldly reality, their ministers set themselves up as cheerleaders for the rebuilding of human society on the model of the ant colony, where individuals matter little so long as collective goals are achieved.

On one policy question after another, mainline Protestant churches today see the state as the source and summit of human action, whose mission trumps the rights of the individual—except, perversely, in the case of sexual autonomy, where these desiccated churches follow the culture in affirming the very sexual "freedoms" their founders considered deadly sins.

The end result of some 150 years of doctrinal erosion, ecclesiastical compromise, and secularizing theology has been not just Progressive Christianity but also the Woke movement in our culture at large.

And the hot burning moral core that drives progressives' outrage is race.

The Last "Christian Moment" in America: The Civil Rights Movement

It is nothing short of startling to consider how the matter (even the definition) of racial justice has changed over the course of two generations—and the role the church has played in promoting that tragic shift.

The civil rights movement was the last great Christian moment in America. It was the final occasion when we as a society drew on Americans' common biblical consensus of what man is and how we should treat him: as a dignified child of God, with rights and responsibilities, equally valuable whatever his traits or state in life.

The Rev. Martin Luther King Jr.'s consistent patriotic and biblical rhetoric, grounding legal equality in America's founding and the Church, helped not just disarm but also shame opponents. While many of his allies and rivals for leadership among black Americans looked to Communism or Islam for help, King knew better. He realized that the civic and religious faith of Americans already rejected racism. All he needed was to show people the implications of what they already believed, not win them over to dismal dialectical materialism or an alien religion founded by a slave owner. It's a vast blessing for our country that real Christian morals, on this issue, won out over primitive white tribalism and fear. For that fact, we have Rev. King to thank.

Things could have gone very differently. For one thing, American apostles of Darwinism had begun the twentieth century weaponizing common racist attitudes to popularize Darwin's theory, and using both to promote eugenics laws. Charles Darwin's defenders today portray the naturalist as having enlightened views on race. As one reviewer summed it up, Darwin's supporters see his theory "a means to unify the races under a common ancestry."[84] But their claims don't hold up. As Darwin scholar Michael Flannery notes,[85] Darwin wrote Rev. Charles Kingsley on February 6, 1862:

> It is very true what you say about the higher races of men, when high enough, replacing & clearing off the lower races. In 500 years how the Anglo-saxon race will have spread & exterminated whole nations; & in consequence how much the Human race, viewed as a unit, will have risen in rank.[86]

This wasn't a momentary lapse on Darwin's part. Nineteen years later he would write to William Graham:

Remember what risks the nations of Europe ran, not so many centuries ago of being overwhelmed by the Turks, and how ridiculous such an idea now is. The more civilised so-called Caucasian races have beaten the Turkish hollow in the struggle for existence. Looking to the world at no very distant date, what an endless number of the lower races will have been eliminated by the higher civilised races throughout the world.[87]

One of Darwin's earliest converts, his cousin Francis Galton, launched the new "science" of eugenics. Its intent? To speed up the evolution of the human species by encouraging the "fit" to survive and breed, and the "unfit" to be sterilized and die off.

Later, in the 1920s, Margaret Sanger founded the American Birth Control League. It is a pro-life commonplace that the American Birth Control League—later rechristened Planned Parenthood—had ties to eugenicists and racists. But that's like saying that the NBA has ties to professional sports. In fact, the birth control movement and the eugenics movement were the same movement. As the classic study of Sanger's crusade, *Blessed Are the Barren*, documents, Margaret Sanger twice tried to merge her organization with major eugenics groups.

The same people served on the boards of the American Eugenics Society and Sanger's organizations for decades. Sanger published many eugenicists in her journal, the *Birth Control Review*. To take only one example, she regularly published

Lothrop Stoddard, a high official of the Massachusetts Ku Klux Klan, whose book *The Rising Tide of Color Against White World Supremacy* Adolf Hitler cited in *Mein Kampf* as "my bible."[88] Sanger invited eugenicists to speak at conferences she organized as well. Thus, she personally approved outrageous and cruel claims about the genetic inferiority of millions of Americans, as well as calls for their forced sterilization and the cut-off of welfare benefits and even private charity to stop the "unfit" from reproducing.

Sanger's organization and eugenicists worked closely together on countless projects, ranging from researching the birth control pill (they tested the early, hazardous versions of the Pill on impoverished rural women in Puerto Rico) to passing forced sterilization or castration laws in more than a dozen states. Those laws targeted blacks and other poor people accused of "feeble mindedness" or "shiftlessness" and diagnosed as "unfit" parents for failing culturally biased IQ tests.[89] The forced-sterilization laws were used to sterilize at least 60,000 Americans and perhaps as many as 200,000.

Sanger herself campaigned tirelessly for eugenics. She saw birth control and eugenics as inseparable. Sanger gave eugenics pep talks at Ku Klux Klan rallies. She wrote articles carrying titles like "Birth Control and Racial Betterment" and "The Eugenic Value of Birth Control." She hailed eugenics for making possible "the breeding out of human weeds—the defective and criminal classes."[90]

In 1934, Sanger issued a call for an "American Baby Code" to incorporate Americans' childbearing decisions into the New

Deal.[91] It would have required married couples to apply for a permit from the federal government before conceiving each new child. The permits would be issued or denied based on eugenic "merit."

In 1932, Sanger gave a major speech in which she called for a "stern and rigid policy of sterilization and segregation to that grade of population whose progeny is already tainted, or whose inheritance is such that objectionable traits may be transmitted to offspring." She concluded the speech by calling on the U.S. government to "apportion farm lands and homestead" to "corral" and "segregate" all the undesirables—"morons, mental defectives, epileptics," as well as "illiterates, paupers, unemployables, criminals, prostitutes, dope-fiends." By Sanger's calculations, this massive concentration camp would house one out of every seven Americans.[92]

Fortunately, Sanger's vision never came to pass in the United States. But one eugenics expert whom Sanger featured as a speaker at a population conference she organized, Eugen Fischer, had run a concentration camp in German-ruled Southwest Africa before World War I. Fischer murdered, starved, and experimented on helpless native Africans. Adolf Hitler read Fischer's book on eugenics; it convinced Hitler of the central importance of eugenics. Another longtime official of Planned Parenthood, Garrett Hardin, had a decades-long track record of serving in eugenics organizations. As late as the 1980s, Hardin was calling for mass forced sterilization of Americans as a necessary solution to the "population problem."

Sanger sought to overcome lingering religious objections to birth control among mainline Protestant elites by stoking the panic that without eugenics laws, "non-Nordics" (i.e., Jews, Southern Europeans, Slavs, and American blacks) would outbreed and overtake the dominance of Anglo-Saxons in America.[93] Strange as it might seem to us today, Sanger made birth control respectable by wrapping it up in racism.

The ranks of eugenicists included Harvard professors, mainline Protestant clergymen, prominent conservationists, for whom entire animal species are named (Madison Grant— he gave his name to a Caribou he discovered, now on display at New York's Museum of Natural History) and the heirs of Gilded Age plutocrats. Much of the funding for eugenics organizations came from the Carnegie Corporation and the Rockefeller Foundation. Supreme Court justice Oliver Wendell Holmes Jr., writing his opinion that the forced sterilization of a supposedly "feeble-minded" woman in Virginia was constitutional, infamously said that "three generations of imbeciles are enough."[94]

It took until 2021 for Planned Parenthood to acknowledge, grudgingly, its long-beloved founder's profoundly racist motivations. Having quite a bit from which to distance themselves, they finally, reluctantly, knocked Sanger from her pedestal.[95]

But Sanger's actions cannot be erased. The powerful documentary *Maafa 21: Black Genocide* plumbs the depths of the movement Sanger helped lead.[96] The film takes its title from the Swahili word for slavery. It contends that the eugenics movement in America began in the panic white racists felt at the end of slavery over what should be done to solve what some called the "Negro problem."

One too-often-forgotten weapon that white elites employed to "manage" minorities was gun control. Southern states that had been forced to release black Americans from slavery turned to restrictions on private firearms. They selectively enforced these restrictions to keep freedmen disarmed. The white leaders who passed and enforced these laws understood that Frederick Douglass has been right in 1863 when he suggested that black Americans would not be "wholly free" until they were equal with the white man not only "at the ballot-box" and "at the jury-box" but also "at the cartridge-box."[97] Disarming black people left them subject to terror tactics from lynch mobs and the Ku Klux Klan. The state-imposed helplessness of black communities subjected them to mob "justice," voter suppression, and unpredictable horrors such as the 1921 Tulsa Race Riot, when armed white vigilantes massacred hundreds of unarmed black citizens and burned down Tulsa's most prosperous black neighborhood.

Nor did racist gun-control tactics end with Jim Crow. In 1968, Congress passed the Gun Control Act. In theory, Congress swung into action after the assassinations of Martin Luther King Jr. and Senator Robert F. Kennedy that year. But other factors may have come into play—namely, the rise of the gun-toting Black Panthers and especially the urban riots that had erupted around the country in 1967 and 1968. In a 1973 book, the left-wing and anti-gun journalist Robert Sherrill wrote bluntly, "The Gun Control Act of 1968 was passed not to control guns but to control blacks." He explained: "Inasmuch as the legislation finally passed in 1968 had nothing to do with the guns used in the assassinations of King and Robert Kennedy, it seems reasonable to assume that the law was directed at that other threat of the 1960s, more omnipresent than the political assassin—namely, the black rioter. . . . With the horrendous rioting of 1967 and 1968, Congress again was panicked toward passing some law that would shut off weapons access to blacks."[98]

Today, black citizens who live in Democrat-controlled cities are subject to rampant crime, but they are hobbled more than most Americans in exercising their Second Amendment right to protect themselves and their property.

Finding New Monsters to Slay

With the ugly reality of laws and practices enforcing racial segregation and preventing "miscegenation," the civil rights movement came as a golden moment in American history. Its leadership was explicitly religious, and its vision of man as the image of God, and thereby endowed with equal dignity, won out over the remnants of popular and elite racism. And it did so by the profoundly Christian tactic of nonviolent civil disobedience on which King had firmly insisted.

In many other countries, inequality didn't end so peacefully. In the late 1960s, the Catholics of Northern Ireland began to protest their unequal treatment. (To be fair, Catholics in the Irish Republic had already hounded most Protestants out.) The common Christianity of the Irish didn't win out. Violent tribalism did. Police brutalized peaceful Catholic demonstrators, who promptly revived the moribund Irish Republican Army. Decades of terrorism on both sides ensued, with armed thugs (Catholic and Protestant) tormenting their communities. That could have happened here. But the civil rights movement was different.

Trouble arose only because many whites (including clergy) who had backed the movement's just demands didn't stop there. The righteous thrill of reforming a nation and changing laws became addictive.

These newly righteous activists went looking for new monsters to slay. Soon the Christians who'd fought racism began to mix with radicals who wanted to tear down much more. For instance, the antiwar movement quickly went past arguments over the prudence of our involvement in Vietnam. Many activists slid into covert, then overt, support of the Communist aggressors in Hanoi.

Others flocked to a "women's liberation" grounded in sexual libertinism and false notions that men and women are interchangeable. The loudest demand of such feminism, and still its central tenet today, was legal abortion—to let women walk away from sexual responsibility, as men could do.

The Christian heart of the civil rights movement fell by the wayside the moment activists no longer needed it. What replaced it? A hunt for any trace of supposed inequality in society, without any further reference to equality's meaning or rational limits. Or why equality even matters. Anti-racism and "social justice" no longer served as mandates imposed by the God of the Bible. They became golden calves instead.

If we really do amount to cosmic accidents produced by random chance, who live a few years and drop like matches into Darwin's toilet, then why even bother with justice and equality? Most primate species are violently hierarchical. It seems to work for them. It worked for pagan civilizations for thousands of years. There are many practical arguments for it. In fact, the only good reason to treat the wildly disparate members of the human race, from Down Syndrome children to supermodels and supergeniuses, as equal is . . . Jesus.

To adopt Darwinian materialism is to sacrifice the right to speak meaningfully of human dignity, rights, or justice.[99] Nature, red in tooth and claw, yawns at those Christian holdovers. Then it licks the fat from its paws. But not many modern people really want to face the black hole at the center of their worldview. They want to cling to the myth that their lives have meaning and their existences some dignity. So they claw at shreds and scraps of the biblical heritage, purloined from the civil rights movement, to patch together systems of ethics.

Christianity, regardless of denomination, has deformed itself for many into a rudderless collectivist grab bag of impulses incompatible with traditional Western reason and freedom—or the basic Christian doctrines concerning God and man that made those freedoms possible.

CHAPTER 4

THE NEW GOSPEL AND
THE GREAT AWOKENING

The Woke movement has for millions taken on both the function and the authority of a traditional religion. But it lacks the core elements of reason or revelation that might constrain its use of power. Progressive Christianity has progressed right past the words and intentions of Christ and become the "new gospel" that Saint Paul warned his disciples against.

While it steals some of its DNA from Christian culture, the Woke movement is a profound perversion of the faith of Jesus of Nazareth. In one passage after another, Jesus asserts his divine authority over the Pharisees by inverting their expectations. He violates the Sabbath, to show that he owns the thing because he decreed it. He mixes with penitent prostitutes and tax collectors and scorns the self-righteous, to emphasize his own centrality, above human customs. He speaks of leaving the ninety-nine "found" sheep to seek the "lost" one. He tells the story of the Prodigal Son, to encourage penitent sinners, and warn the self-satisfied, like the elder brother.

All these stories make sense, and point to genuine orthodox Christianity, if we understand them properly—as Christ insisting on his divine authority and offering mercy from the Father. To keep that meaning, we need to remember some other things Jesus said. For instance, that he had come "not to abolish the Law, but fulfill it." That is, he spoke in perfect continuity with the Hebrew scriptures (the only ones in existence at the time). He came first to the "lost sheep" of Israel. The Gospel must be preached first to the Jews.

The vision of life in the Hebrew Bible which God offers as a reward for faithfulness cannot be evil, as Progressive theologians imply. That vision includes economic prosperity, secure property rights, heterosexual marriage, firm national borders, and hierarchical differences as the result of different levels of talent. Any version of Christianity which claims that Jesus pronounced such things as damnable sets him as hopelessly opposed to his own Father.

But what if we cut the New Testament off from the Old? If we treat Jesus almost as a new God who'd come to rescue us from the "judgmentalism" and "wrath" of the Father? That temptation to bifurcate the Bible popped up early in Church history and has resurfaced again and again ever since. What better way, some Christians seem to think, to emphasize Jesus' uniqueness than to push their interpretation of his words and deeds to the wildest extreme? Highlight and celebrate Christianity's differences from Judaism by refusing even to see his works in their Jewish context. Instead interpret them "radically" and make them an ideology. Embrace the most counterintuitive and even irrational implications we can draw to prove that we honor faith over reason.

It's not enough to assert that women are morally equal to men. We must insist that men and women are interchangeable, in fact mere "social constructions." A polyamorous drag queen is "equally" fit to teach our young children as a faithfully married Christian or a celibate nun. We must give hulking, bearded boys the "equal" chance to knock out teenage girls on the rugby field. If authentically (that is *biologically*) male rapists wish to transfer to women's prisons, denying them that is "equal" to forcing black American Christians to drink from different water fountains.

To offer some armature of rational theory for the frenzied advancement of indiscriminate "equality," Progressives turn to the academic movement called Intersectionality. As even gay liberal journalist Andrew Sullivan described it:

> "Intersectionality" is the latest academic craze sweeping the American academy. On the surface, it's a recent neo-Marxist theory that argues that social oppression does not simply apply to single categories of identity—such as race, gender, sexual

orientation, class, etc.—but to all of them in an interlocking system of hierarchy and power.[100]

And it's our job as good citizens, seeking justice and equality (despite Darwin's apparent debunking of both concepts), to root out oppression wherever we think we've found it. Far more than a job, it's a vocation, the salvation project of a new, post-Christian religion: the Woke cult. I use the word "cult" advisedly, since this intensely moralistic movement closely mimics some aspects of traditional Christian practice and psychology.

Followers of the Woke cult discover that the world is deeply wrong. It is permeated by evil—the evil of inequality. And that evil has an author: straight white males. Realizing the depth and extent of this all-pervading evil comes as a kind of conversion. One wakes up. Then one is "woke." That's Social Justice Warrior (SJW)-speak for "saved." Hence, the first moment of faith. "I once was lost but now am found. / Was blind but now I see."

If a person belongs to any other group but straight white males, then she is in luck: She's certified as a victim. She deserves special treatment from everyone from college deans to government bureaucrats. Even better, she should feel virtuous for wallowing in anger and resentment. No matter if she's Malia Obama. She can righteously seethe with rage at jobless white coal miners or homeless white veterans. Her sense of victimhood gives her the "blessed assurance" that she is part of the Elect.

Go deeper into the cult and the disciplines get more rigorous. Now white women must admit their role in oppressing women of color. This requires some of the groveling expected of white males. But it offers the same benefit: a sense of forgiveness and spiritual progress. Likewise, black males must atone to women of color. All straights must bow down to gays. Even gays must make amends for their insensitivity to "trans" people. I am not sure to whom "trans" people of color must apologize. But give intellectuals time and they'll find someone. Or invent him.

This new religious movement apes the structure of a Christian conversion and of subsequent life in the Spirit. It does so, of course, at a much shallower level. It replaces worship with protest. Spirituality with unhinged histrionics. Examination of conscience with the scapegoating of others conveniently dead or out of power.

This creed also mimics Christian salvation history. The straight white male is the phallic serpent in the Garden. In one place after another (especially in the Americas), these oppressors discovered a prelapsarian paradise. And in each case, we paved it and made it a parking lot.

To keep up this myth of the Fall, and its tempter, Progressives have to ignore a lot of facts. They have to whitewash:

- The fact of Arab-run slavery in Africa before Europeans arrived.[101]
- The cruelties and slaughters of the Muslim conquests from Spain to India.[102]

- The savage wars, routine torture, and environmental devastation that marked the lives of North American Indians.[103]
- The ritual cannibalism practiced by the genocidal Aztecs.[104]
- The theological tyranny upper-class Hindus wielded over millions of "untouchables."[105]

Likewise in sexual politics, social justice warriors must wish away:

- The brutal cost of abortion in innocent lives and women's mental health.[106]
- The collapse of the human birthrate everywhere that feminism has arrived.[107]
- The decline of marriage and the explosion of single mothers dependent on the government.[108]
- The obsession of gay male culture with promiscuity and youth, including underage boys.[109]
- The abundant evidence that biological sex is real and "trans" fantasies are symptoms of mental illness.[110]

Accepting any of these facts would shatter the sweet certitude of a life of faith. Those who try to speak of them commit blasphemy. So believers must flee the occasion of sin— or better yet, expel the unbeliever.

You can't really argue with zealots like this. They've constructed a palace of funhouse mirrors in which to live. Their new, fantastic religion takes up all the space where real faith in Christ could live.

Welcome to the Great Awokening.

Accepting Caesar as Your Personal Lord and Savior

Many of the activists who support these new, outrageous movements still consider themselves Christians. Of course, they might modify the term, to distinguish themselves clearly from "zealots" whom they detest. The typical term is "progressive," though "inclusive" and "welcoming" also make their appearances. These radical new social crusades that march through the culture rely on the legacy of the civil rights movement for its legitimacy. By defending the claims of newly minted "victim" groups, partisans fancy that they are following in the tradition of Rev. Martin Luther King and the millions of orthodox Christians who came to support him. They see that the decisions of courts (such as *Brown v. Board of Education*) and the passage of federal legislation (e.g., the Civil Rights Act) helped to root out grave evils which Christians condemn.

Sadly, this reinforces within churches a belief in the central tenet of the Social Gospel—the claim that *the state is the primary means of achieving God's work on earth*. Now, in many cases it's necessary for Christians to engage in political action, as the pro-life movement recognizes. But the shift of emphasis in churches to political lobbying from personal evangelism and private charity profoundly threatens religious vitality. To cite a chilling example, while the sex abuse crisis was in full force, devastating my own Catholic Church, our Catholic bishops conference was busy churning out hundreds of public policy white papers on issues ranging from immigration to welfare spending, as if it were the legitimate U.S. government in exile. Of course, among those political demands the bishops made were calls for more and stricter control of private firearms. The only cure for crime and disorder—or anything else—is that messianic force in human history, the U.S. federal government.

Or even worse, global government, via superstates like the European Union, newly empowered UN agencies, and transnational for-profit companies like Google, Facebook, Disney, and other Woke corporations that increasingly act like autocratic governments, policing private opinion and punishing citizens who dare to express the "wrong" views.

Purges

The genuine justification that traditional Christian faith offers is a powerful thing. It infuses the soul and unites us to Christ even in the midst of this veil of tears. The conviction that we follow and try to spread the one true religion of the Creator of the Universe—from the Big Bang to the bacterium, from the farthest-flung galaxy to subatomic particles . . . that changes people. It produces self-emptying apostles like Saint Paul and Dietrich Bonhoeffer. It forms humble, courageous scholars, such as Saints Augustine and Anselm. It permits great humanitarians, such as William Wilberforce and Mother

Cabrini, to grow out of such acorns of faith, sheltering millions from suffering.

But get it a little twisted and that conviction of faith also generates inquisitors, witch burners, and bigots. Confuse your own ego with the "honor of God" and you can become a monster. The stern moral code at the heart of orthodox faith provides a brake on such tendencies, and the same Christian world that produced religious persecution also discovered that religious freedom lies at the core of human dignity. The conviction of our own sinfulness and utter dependence on God, at Christianity's hot beating heart, should give a bad conscience to the most self-righteous fanatic.

None of these restraints hobbles the Woke. In fact, Progressive Christians convince themselves that they are more Christian than Jesus. They imagine that they have advanced beyond every previous generation of believer, and treat Christ's own words the way that He (the Incarnate God) handled the Old Testament. The letter of Christ's commands kills, while the Progressive spirit gives life. As my Progressive high school religion teacher once sneered to me: "Jesus didn't have an MA in theology from Catholic University. I do."

Nor do the Woke let reason restrain them. They have studied the cynical theories of French philosophers like Jacques Derrida and Michel Foucault, and embraced a hermeneutic of suspicion toward all past wisdom. They'd even smash reason's tools such as logic, empirical science, and mathematics. Instead of trying to stand on the shoulders of giants, the Woke pretend that they've found their vast feet of clay. Such thinkers were "white males," you see. With all the vulgar hubris of Nazi race-cranks sneering at Einstein's "Jewish science," the Woke exempt themselves from learning and exalt their own willful ignorance. They crawl into their bunker and move little flags around on maps, winning imaginary victories.

Once your ideology has convinced you that your fellow citizens are hardly-human moral monsters, you'll be terrified of them, and your own sense of self-preservation will goad you to maximum ruthlessness. That in turn will feed your obsession with gaining and wielding power. Your scruples will slough away, as you see the circle of good, enlightened people surrounded and endangered. With your self-righteous ego puffed up by an utterly unearned sense of moral superiority over every previous human generation, you yourself are the danger. But, of course, you can't see this, can you? You're an unhinged and unreflective zealot, like any that ever ran a concentration camp.

Once enough citizens have mentally deformed themselves this way, they seamlessly support intense repression of any dissent. The Left won't live and let live. Its leaders and institutions waged a 60-year revolutionary struggle against Christian, middle-class culture. Because so many leaders of the right proved easy to cow, or bribe, or swindle, the Left has triumphed. Completely, except for a few pockets of resistance here and there.

And now the revolutionaries have resolved to fully impose their power over us. This means that they aim to purge every nook and cranny of private or public life, from school to church to home, in all 50 states of the Union, with no hint of mercy. Our leaders turned out as corrupt and bumbling as the generals in South Vietnam. The elites in South Vietnam lived at vast distance from the people they claimed to govern. In other words, they held their governing base in contempt, as GOP leaders felt about Donald Trump and his supporters. South Vietnam's leaders often squandered the money the U.S. gave them, pocketing much of it. Their generals stayed far away from the front lines of battle, and chose commanding officers based not on their competence, but cronyism. Just so, too many in the GOP kept far away from our efforts to demand an honest election in 2020.

The radical left prevailed in Vietnam for the same reasons they're prevailing here. The Communists in Vietnam on both sides of the border were ideologically disciplined, intolerant, and ruthless. So the U.S. Left has shown itself since 2016, from the street thugs of Antifa all the way to the talking heads on CNN, and the cadres of 22-year-olds with degrees in Queer Theory who censor epidemiologists on Facebook.

Meanwhile, many of those who claim to be the opposition, the defenders of freedom, can be bought off or scared off. What happened to all those Republican governors, secretaries of state, and state legislators whose job it was to ensure a fair election between Joe Biden and Donald Trump? They failed in their duties to our Constitution and our country, as surely as did those generals who jetted out of Saigon in 1975 with suitcases full of cash.

And the Left's victorious cadres have proven as intolerant and fanatical as the North Vietnamese who stormed into

Saigon. We are to be re-educated, and those who resist will be destroyed. This means from top to bottom. Any conservative leader, or business, or activist, who rises out of obscurity and succeeds will be targeted and ruined. The Left will accomplish this in a coordinated fashion, via censorship, boycotts, smear campaigns, and if need be through street violence by mobs. Sadly, you can count on our remaining "leaders" to . . . panic and try to collaborate with our enemies. They'll toss our wounded over the side to the crocodiles, in the hopes of getting eaten last.

The Republican leaders in Congress who went along with the fantasy narrative that the January 6 selfie-fest at the Capitol was really the Reichstag Fire were only the worst offenders. Before that, think of how the same Republicans joined the *New York Times*-led smear campaign against Rep. Steve King. Or how the same "conservatives" in Congress have treated Rep. Lauren Boebert? (Compare that to how the Democrats rally behind representatives Ilhan Omar and Alexandria Ocasio-Cortez, no matter how radical their outbursts.) Remember how *National Review* led the cannibalistic feeding frenzy against Nick Sandmann? The list of sellouts and betrayals goes on and on.

The campaign to squelch, crush, and silence us is comprehensive, and extends to every level of society. No one is immune. Not self-made multimillionaires like Mike Lindell (the CEO of My Pillow), nor successful conservative media companies such as the utterly non-extremist conservative video channel Prager U—which, as I write, is being kicked off its media servers.

The Left demands unconditional surrender, and a thorough-going purge. Since everything they dislike is somehow "racist," it might as well be "Nazi." And what do we do with Nazis? Hang them when we can, but in the meantime punch them, silence them, try to ruin their lives and careers.

That really is the level of moral discernment and nuance the Left is preaching at Ivy League colleges and inside government agencies. These people have decided that America needs de-Nazification. One of Joe Biden's first actions in office was to appoint Bishop Garrison, an advocate of Marxist "Critical Race Theory," to purge the U.S. military of "extremists" such as evangelical Christians and orthodox Catholics.[111] As *Revolver News* reported, "Garrison called the entire concept of free speech itself in the information age a 'digital black plague' that will usher in a 'modern day dark age' if not reined in by censorship."[112]

Treating PTA Moms as Domestic Terrorists

Not even ordinary parents in obscure American suburbs can live in peace. The "little platoons" that Edmund Burke and Alexis de Tocqueville identified as the backbone of ordered liberty? They must be crushed. That's the only explanation for what happened to New Hampshire wife and mother Shannon McGinley in 2021. You see, Mrs. McGinley apparently committed a war crime: as a conservative Christian, she tried to help out at her kids' private school.

As the *NH Journal* reported:

> A group of Derryfield School alums, led by activists in Los Angeles and Washington, D.C., is pushing the prep school to kick a local mom off the Board of Trustees because of her advocacy on behalf of her religious beliefs.
>
> Shannon McGinley is well known in New Hampshire political circles as executive director of Cornerstone, a traditional Christian organization. She's also a mother of five who has had children at Derryfield since 2009. McGinley has served on the board for eight years and is currently its secretary.
>
> McGinley was taken aback to learn she was the lead topic on comedian/activist Sarah Silverman's podcast. . . . Silverman, a Bedford, N.H. native and Derryfield alum, mistakenly declared McGinley the "executive director of a gay conversion center in New Hampshire."
>
> Silverman went on to argue that McGinley should be kicked off the board for the views she holds ("Are we deciding bigotry is an opinion?").[113]

So Silverman's many followers were solemnly informed that Mrs. McGinley runs some kind of cruel reeducation camp where (legend tells) unwilling gay kids are subject to Cuban-style brainwashing or something. If that were true, it would be alarming. But it isn't. No such "gay conversion center" exists in New Hampshire, or ever has existed. McGinley has no connection with any such institution. She did oppose a bill that purported to ban "gay conversion therapy," but that was because the bill would have prevented gay Christians from voluntarily getting professional help informed by Christian faith. The Progressive activists who led the campaign to oust McGinley from the school board included a former staffer on Democrat Pete Buttigieg's 2020 presidential campaign. Silverman took her own shaky grasp of the agitprop and ran with it.

Never mind that McGinley had served faithfully on the Derryfield board for eight years, with zero complaints about anything to do with LGBT students. As the campaign against her intensified, McGinley wrote her friends and colleagues on the board:

> I am writing in response to demands that I be removed from The Derryfield School Board of Trustees because I hold to and promote Catholic teachings on gender, sexuality, and marriage. I am of course saddened that I am facing a discriminatory and hateful personal attack. But I am far more troubled by the possibility that the school I

have loved for many years may capitulate to these demands—an act that would reward intolerance and set an example of bigotry to the students and community I care deeply about. . . .

[T]hose attacking me not only believe in legally sanctioning speech they disagree with but in systematically removing those like me from civil society for opposing them. I invite you to ask yourselves whether their monolithic intolerance or my religious faith is more compatible with Derryfield's commitment to diversity.[114]

It's worth trying to hold the left to its own hypocritical claims. But don't get your hopes up. We know perfectly well that apart from ethnic and sexual bean counting, leftists don't believe in "diversity." They want uniformity, perfect accord of the kind found in termite colonies and promised in totalitarian Utopias.

The Derryfield board did capitulate. They removed Shannon McGinley.

The Original Sin: Racism

The intolerant left claims the moral high ground on the basis of "racism." Every other "phobia" and "ism" that the left denounces ("Islamophobia," "heterosexism," "transphobia") gains rhetorical power by its analogy to racism, which was all too real. Every time a Republican tries to enforce our binding, democratically enacted (and once bipartisan) immigration laws, commentators will compare the arrest of illegal immigrants to the assaults on civil rights workers in 1950s Alabama. (Of course, they tend to turn a blind eye when a Progressive is involved. Case in point: Michelle Obama condemned the Trump administration throwing children detained at the border "into cages." Mrs. Obama failed to mention, and few in the legacy media bothered to point out, that her own husband's administration had built those "cages."[115])

We Americans are genuinely and rightly ashamed of the institution of slavery and of the systematic segregation and discrimination that followed it. But pseudo- and quasi-scientific movements weaponized that real racism, and today's "anti-racism" has little in common with the claims Rev. Martin Luther King Jr. made for black Americans. Instead, dismissing the very documents to which King pointed as sources for his demand for equal treatment under law, new movements such as Critical Race Theory rest on Marxist methodology.

The 1619 Project proves it.

The Protocols of the Elders of Jamestown

What would you think if a major newspaper published an elaborate, fanciful conspiracy theory? And if it implicated one ethnic group with racial guilt, such that we shouldn't trust its members? And if major national institutions colluded in creating the conspiracy theory to whip up racial resentment and gain political power?

Let's say this theory got important facts wrong, or simply made them up in the hope that no one would check them. It cast a whole nation in moral disgrace. It contributed to a campaign to dehumanize one race—because that race was supposedly rich, privileged, and habitually wicked. What if zealots lapped up this theory and used it to warp the minds of children in school?

This is not fantasy. I'm describing two real but separate documents, more than a hundred years apart: *The Protocols of the Elders of Zion* and the 1619 Project.

Each document pretended that it had unearthed historical secrets. The *Protocols* claimed to expose a global Jewish conspiracy, purporting to be the transcript of meetings in which Jewish leaders laid out secret plans to afflict Gentile nations with all the evils of modernity, everything from sexual promiscuity and disruptive capitalism to revolutionary movements. The 1619 Project pretends that it can explain America's whole history as the fruits of a white racist conspiracy. Start with the European settlement, then the American Revolution, and then the rise of capitalism. The authors assert that America's true founding came not in 1620 with the Mayflower Compact, nor in 1776 with the Declaration of Independence, but in 1619, when the first black slaves arrived in Jamestown, Virginia.

The *Protocols* claimed to expose systemic Jewish subversion as the motor of world events. The 1619 Project makes similar claims for systemic white racism. (This despite the fact that slavery was practiced worldwide in 1619 but didn't seem to generate capitalism or constitutional government in, say, the Ottoman Empire.) The 1619 Project's most shocking claim? That the thirteen colonies declared independence mainly out of fear that King George III planned to free their slaves.

This is, quite simply, wrong. Many prominent scholars denounced the 1619 Project as at heart politicized fiction. Several historians who have documented the real evils of slavery wrote a letter to the *New York Times* expressing their concerns about the "factual errors in the project." The letter's signers included well-known liberals Sean Wilentz, Gordon Wood, and James McPherson, all award-winning historians.[116] The *Times* responded by writing, "We don't believe that the request for corrections to The 1619 Project is warranted." But as historian Philip Magness pointed out, when fact checks did appear, the *Times* would flout journalistic standards by making "stealth-edits" to the text of the Project, shoving its discredited claims down George Orwell's "memory hole."[117]

The *Protocols* were a forgery, of course. First appearing in a Russian newspaper in 1903, they may have been the work of the tsar's secret police, who wished to discredit revolutionaries as tools of "the Jews." Whatever their origin, the *Protocols* spread all over the world. In the United States, pioneering automaker Henry Ford use his newspaper, the *Dearborn Independent*, to publish a series of articles that cited the *Protocols*. Later, Ford collected those articles into a book titled *The International Jew: The World's Foremost Problem*. The book was translated into sixteen languages and earned praise from Adolf Hitler and Joseph Goebbels.[118]

But the truth came out. As *The Holocaust Encyclopedia* recounts:

> In 1921, the *London Times* presented conclusive proof that the *Protocols* was a "clumsy plagiarism." The *Times* confirmed that the *Protocols* had been copied in large part from a French political satire that never mentioned Jews—Maurice Joly's *Dialogue in Hell Between Machiavelli and Montesquieu* (1864). Other investigations revealed that one chapter of a Prussian novel, Hermann Goedsche's *Biarritz* (1868), also "inspired" the *Protocols*.[119]

Alas, the exposure of these facts didn't get the *Protocols* shoved into bookstores' "Fantasy" sections. The Nazis and their allies pretended that the work was never discredited. In some squalid circles you still see it cited. Arabic editions still sell briskly.

Given that it was generated in the very cradle of elite opinion and messianic belief, the 1619 Project will surely have a similarly long and destructive life. Soon after its appearance, its authors received the once-coveted Pulitzer Prize. *The New York Times* has created lesson plans for teachers to use in history classrooms nationwide. Leftist teachers unions and education bureaucrats are teaching the Project as inarguable fact in blue states and cities nationwide.

Nor is the 1619 Project some isolated crank pamphlet. Instead, it provides (as the *Protocols* did) the "factual" basis for a campaign of hatred, resentment, and political demands aimed at members of just one race. With corporations forcing white employees to sit through "diversity training" that talks about "toxic whiteness" and "white fragility," bad history has evil consequences.

It even leads to violence in the streets. In June 2020, Claremont McKenna College professor Charles Kesler wrote a *New York Post* column in which he suggested that the George Floyd riots should be called the "1619 Riots."[120] The lead author of the 1619 Project, Nikole Hannah-Jones, didn't object. On the contrary, Hannah-Jones retweeted Kesler's piece and wrote: "It would be an honor. Thank you."[121]

Meanwhile, key Evangelical bodies such as the Southern Baptist Convention have succumbed to pressure to incorporate Critical Race Theory in seminaries and schools. These churches seem unconcerned about a method of studying history that has its origin in Marxist movements such as Black Liberation Theology. Although those movements are incompatible with, even uninterested in, orthodox Christianity, the churches apparently view the move as a means of atoning for genuine past evils—such as the support for slavery among key founders of that denomination. But how exactly does that work? Those Baptists who backed the Confederacy were rejecting the equality promised by the Declaration of Independence and the increasing limits on the expansion of slavery favored by the Unionists. In what way does explaining away the Declaration (and indeed the whole American Founding) as equally racist "make up" for those dead men's sins? If anything, supporters of Critical Race Theory agree with the Confederates that the United States was founded as a "white man's nation," with slavery as a central institution, not a profound moral anomaly that must someday be expunged.

Nor can we count on elites in the Catholic Church to offer us solid guidance. Under Pope Francis, the Vatican has transformed itself into little more than a Kantian NGO with a gift shop. It is committed to wealth redistribution and globalist government. It has even allied itself with Communist China[122]—from which it reportedly received $2 billion per year in exchange for its silence about the persecution of Christians and the genocide of Uyghur Muslims.[123] From those millions of peaceful Muslims now in Chinese concentration camps, China steals human organs from both the dead and the living, as *Forbes* magazine reported, and sells them for profit.[124]

Bishop Marcelo Sanchez Sorondo—the Vatican's top authority on Catholic social teaching, and a close aide to Pope Francis—toured China in late 2019. With Communist Party minders carefully shepherding Bishop Sorondo, the tour called to mind the pilgrimages intellectuals and clergymen once took to Stalin's Russia. Those Western Progressives returned full of praise for the Soviets' accomplishments. Similarly, Bishop Sorondo declared, "Pope Francis has love and confidence in China; and China trusts Pope Francis."[125]

By that time, the Vatican had handed control of the Chinese church to Communist Party puppets. The pope recognized bishops Beijing had appointed without Vatican approval. The Vatican had excommunicated the bishops previously. With this deal, the Vatican sold out the loyal Catholics of China who refused to bow to the Communist regime's "Catholic Patriotic Association." Cardinal Joseph Zen, the former archbishop of Hong Kong, called the deal "an incredible betrayal," adding, "A church enslaved by the government is no real Catholic Church."[126] Although the deal increased the persecution of Christians in China,[127] Bishop Sorondo went even further during his China visit. He called for the Vatican to reestablish diplomatic relations with China's totalitarian Communist regime.

So, as you can see, we're on our own. Certainly, Christians have all the great resources of two millennia of prayer, reflection, and debate over the meaning of the Bible, and the proper interaction between faith and reason. But we can't count on our leaders. We'll have to do our own research, find sound and reliable preachers, and carefully choose among our congregations to find those we can trust. Most of all, as individual believers we will need to discern how to apply the deep truths of natural law and the real implications of Christian ethics to everyday, emerging concerns.

To do that, we'll need a strong grasp of how previous faithful believers have struggled in their time with similar questions. In other words, we must understand tradition. We will also need solid ground rules for how to reason about questions of faith. Most of all, we must cultivate a spirit of skepticism and resistance at a time when the world seems increasingly bent on carving up the Gospel into fashionable shapes and painting it in trendy colors. We'll need to know which hills are worth dying on.

PART II

RULES FOR RATIONAL
CHRISTIANS

CHAPTER 5

THE HARMONY OF THE OLD TESTAMENT AND THE NEW

Let me tell you the story of Christianity's first major doctrinal crisis, its first important heresy.[128]

The Christian thinker Marcion (b. 110) was brilliant, austere, and pious. His father was a very prominent pastor (a bishop, in fact). He brought with him a huge personal fortune, which he laid at the feet of the Church in a time of persecution. But Marcion offered something even more attractive: clear and simple solutions. At a time when the Church was wrestling with interminable confusions, Marcion had answers.

There was just one problem: They were the kind of answers that Woke Christians offer our churches today.

Putting the Bible Under the Knife

The greatest conundrum the early Church faced was reckoning with the Old Testament. In Marcion's time, the second century, there were still more Jews than Christians spread through the Roman Empire. These people laid prior claim to the Hebrew Bible and denied what Christians made of it. Many descendants of Gentile Christians looked askance at believers of Jewish descent. Did they still wish to "judaize" the Church, burdening new converts (contra Saint Paul) with outdated traditions? Doubtless an element of what we might call "Gentile nationalism," or plain resentment, was at work in some of that "anti-Judaism."

Beyond all that, the text of the Old Testament proved a stumbling block to philosophically minded pagans, whom Christians wished to convert. It was one thing to point to Jesus as the Logos when speaking to Greek Neo-Platonists. It was quite another to explain to them how "Thou Shalt Not Kill" could be reconciled with Joshua's conquest of Canaan. Or the injunction to hunt down the Amalekites. Or the instances when God was said to experience "wrath," then afterward "repented himself."

Jesus spoke of the Father almost constantly, and only in a few crucial passages had he laid claim to divinity. On many occasions he'd asserted his authority by flouting the letter of the Jewish law. But he'd also insisted that he came to fulfill it, not abolish it. The Jews denied that he had. The Gentiles didn't see why he'd bothered. They looked at God as revealed in the Hebrew scriptures as inscrutable and imperfect, hardly the tranquil First Cause suggested by Aristotle.

The real task of the Church was to discern which elements of the Old Testament were unchangeable, essential, and universal for all God's creatures—including those Gentiles now considering Christian faith. How to situate the new revelations of Jesus in the context of such timeless truths? How should we preach to them in an unbelieving and hostile world without conceding anything crucial?

As Christians today, we face an analogous task: how to preserve the fundamental truths of the faith while answering the claims of a post-Christian world. To post-modern intellectuals, the historic teachings of the Church often seem as repugnant as the Old Testament doctrines did to "enlightened" Greeks in Marcion's time.

Struggling with such paradoxes took the early Church several centuries of fervent debate and careful discernment by her very best minds. (We now call them the Church's "Fathers.") Along the way, many heresies would emerge to divide a Church still being hunted by the Romans. Poor Constantine, who finally offered tolerance and even favor to the Church, would promptly face a bitter split between those who asserted Jesus's full, coequal divinity and those who denied it. He'd convene the Council of Nicaea to try to resolve it.

What if it could all be much, much simpler? Marcion thought so. He looked at the tangle of claims made by pro- and anti-"judaizers" and found a straightforward answer. According to legend, Alexander the Great had walked up to the famous

Gordian Knot, a convoluted and inextricable tangle of rope. Told that the man who solved it would conquer Asia, Alexander drew his sword and sliced straight through.

Eager to conquer the Church (on arriving in Rome, he demanded to be made a bishop), Marcion did the same. Faced with the difficulties of the Old Testament, he sliced it off. Marcion declared the "God" of the Hebrew Bible unworthy of Jesus's "higher" and "purer" ethics. He announced that the Father of whom Jesus spoke was not the entity who'd spoken to Abraham and Moses, but some vastly more elevated God. The "lesser" god of the Jews, Marcion declared, was some well-meaning but bumbling "demiurge." The true God, whom Jesus had come to declare, wished to set us free—from the countless demands of the Old Testament, from its god, and from the Jews.

Faced with Gospels and apostolic letters that contradicted his theory, Marcion cut them off, too. He accepted just one gospel, Saint Luke's, and only in the "corrected" form he edited and published. He picked just ten of Saint Paul's letters, then tossed out all the rest of the New Testament. His prophetic insight into the authentic "spirit" of Christianity gave life, while the letter killed.

This new, user-friendly version of Christianity spread through the Mediterranean like kudzu through Alabama. It was much, much easier for Greeks and Romans to accept. It required no concessions whatsoever to Jewish scriptures, which Marcion cast off as the tribal creed of a second-tier deity. It solved the complexities of Jesus's nature by denying his humanity. Jesus wasn't incarnate as both the Yahweh of the Jews and a Jewish carpenter's stepson. Instead, he was merely a "manifestation" of some higher, cosmic God.

Marcionite Christianity fit perfectly with the philosophic opinions and cultural attitudes of the age. And for a very good reason: it was their product. Instead of a full, rich tradition that went back for thousands of years as the revelation of God, the creed of Marcion was the fruit of exquisite plastic surgery so extreme it would put today's transgender clinics to shame.

Although Marcion's movement may seemingly have vanished, its spirit just went underground. His method has proved a go-to tactic whenever a group of Christians wanted to free itself to think bold new thoughts. Uplifting, inspiring thoughts that the Church had already rejected. For instance, it became the instrument by which to promote absolute pacifism, the rejection of capital punishment, and the end of private property.

The scholar Hans Urs von Balthasar wrote about how the secularizing thinkers of the Enlightenment wanted to win over Christians.[129] Philosophical radicals such as Hegel and Percy Bysshe Shelley liked what they called the "spirit" of Christianity, but they wanted to blot out the letter. They kept running up against orthodox takes on scripture that blocked their road to Utopia. Such traditional readings of the New Testament interpreted it through the Old. They harmonized Jesus's teachings with the Father's, preventing radical interpretations that suited the fancies of armchair social engineers.

So those Enlightenment thinkers adopted the spirit of Marcion. They painted Jesus as a liberator from the harsh, inhuman norms . . . of his very own Father. They weaponized anti-Semitism to help sell their case to the reading public.

The Marcionite impulse keeps popping up over the centuries. Whenever some Christians feel the Gnostic impulse to denigrate Creation, they reinvent Marcionite teachings— more "elevated" and "purer" than the mere Orthodoxy preached by the Church. When the Nazis convinced Christian churches that Jews were the root of all evil, tame theologians stepped up to rehabilitate Marcion himself.

How to Be More Christian than Jesus

And today we face Marcionism in an updated, virulent form. Progressive Christians seem perfectly happy to offer the Marcionite sex change (snip here, snip there) to the Church's historic doctrines. They shed most of the Old Testament especially. It contains those pesky prohibitions of most sexual sins, as well as firm endorsements of national borders, private property, and the "patriarchal" family.

Progressives will take their surgical scissors to the New Testament, too—even Christ's own words. Their hazy, idiosyncratic ideas about "what a Good God would really do" become their highest religious authority. Which means that their own notions—formed by a secular culture, intellectual fashions, and fear of being labeled "reactionary" or "Christian nationalist"— sit on the teaching throne like a private pope. So Progressives go past the dead letter of Jesus's own words and deeds to find their secret spirit. Wise modern scholars (just like the Gnostics) are eager to help.

At every point where the Gospel itself stands athwart the project of post-modern sexual freedom and this-worldly salvation via the government, Marcion shows up, smiling. Surely, he suggests, that if Jesus were alive today, he'd approve of:

- Same-sex marriage and even polyamory.
- Sex change operations and puberty blockers for teens.
- Explicit sex ed for kids.
- Drag queen story hour at public libraries featuring sex offenders.
- Honoring the "forest gods" of Amazon natives as a source of divine revelation.
- Rejecting affordable energy and placing control of our heat, light, and movement from place to place in the hands of global bureaucrats.
- Disobeying Caesar and smuggling illegal immigrants, then profiting off federal contracts to provide them tax-funded benefits.
- Flooding Christian countries with Muslims who favor sharia, and hence the persecution of the Church.
- Legal abortion.

- The use of organs carved out from the living bodies of fetuses in vaccines and virus research.

- Heavily taxing working people to support a permanent class of dependents, who sell their votes to the party of big government in return for bread and circuses.

- Confiscating citizens' guns, rendering them completely dependent on Caesar for protection against violent crime and defenseless against any mob violence and possible future tyranny.

All these are the stances essential to making important friends these days, to gaining the respect of the "wise ones," and in some places to avoiding the ire of Caesar. Surely holding these views is what Jesus expects, isn't it? No, it's not part of what he literally said. But Marcion has taught us how to read between the lines.

CHAPTER 6

THE GOLDEN MEAN

One of the most venerable maxims in Western philosophy is to pursue moderation in all aspects of life. In his ethics, Aristotle codified this Socratic injunction in the phrase "The Golden Mean." By this, he meant what we'd call the "sweet spot," the ideal and balanced approach to every moral question and personal habit. This doesn't mean we must be lukewarm toward everything, or especially the important things. In fact, Jesus warned against that, saying that he'd "spit out" those who only moderately loved God.

But how do we love God and all the things he made? In due proportion, and in proper measure, and in tension with each other. We love our friends, and we love our country. But what if one of our friends betrays the country? Or commits a heinous crime? That's just a stark instance of the regular tensions that emerge among the various things we love.

To determine how to properly love things, to treat each of them justly—giving each person and thing its due, no more and no less—is the study of a lifetime. To manage that is to practice what Aristotle and St. Thomas Aquinas called the highest natural virtue: prudence. That word doesn't mean "timidity" or "pragmatism," though sometimes cowardly or unprincipled people hide behind it. A soldier who loves his comrades and decides to throw himself on a grenade to save them might very well be acting prudently. The soldier who hides from combat, or foolishly runs into No Man's Land and dies, is not. Prudence requires that we seek out the truth of a situation, justly weigh varying claims, and then act courageously but temperately.

The reason we have and need a system of justice is to rectify imbalances that emerge as fallen people strive to obtain what each thinks is his due, and to discern by objective, valid standards based on reason who genuinely deserves what.

Likewise, in our practice of the moral life, as fallen creatures with limited knowledge, we face constant temptations affecting each of our natural gifts and faculties. We can employ them to excess, or totally neglect them. One of my previous books— and frankly, my favorite—is called *The Bad Catholic's Guide to the Seven Deadly Sins*. Most books on that subject lay out only the deadly sins and the virtues we ought to practice instead. But that's incomplete. Because the opposite of each deadly sin is not in fact a virtue—it's a dangerous overcorrection against it, which is in itself a sin.

You can divvy up the whole moral life among seven faculties that God gave us to sustain us as social, rational animals. (Think of them as "talents." How well are we investing them? Are they buried in the yard?). Here they are, listed, each with the Deadly Sin that can emerge when we pervert them.

- Sexuality (Lust)
- Aggression (Wrath)
- Nutrition (Gluttony)
- Acquisitiveness (Greed)
- Productivity (Sloth)
- Self-Reflection (Vanity)
- Sociability (Envy)

It's not hard to see how each of the deadly sins is an abuse, overuse, or distortion of each of these faculties. Many earnest believers think that if a sin is so deadly it made the list, the safe thing to do is to err as far as possible in the opposite direction. But that's like throwing the switch on the water in your shower from freezing to boiling—not a wise idea. Embracing over-corrections as virtues is the source of much of the dysfunction, weirdness, and ineffectuality we encounter in Christian circles—and of many "radical" stances taken by Christians that don't do justice to people, their God-given dignity, or what they need to live freely and well.

Overcorrecting against the Seven Deadly Sins can lead to what we might call the Seven Deadly Neuroses. Here's how those neuroses look when compared with the relevant sins as well as the moderate virtues:

- You might indulge in the deadly sin of **Lust** and engage in or obsess about illicit sex. Or if you've mastered **Chastity**, you confine its use to its proper context, marriage. If you are consumed by fear of sin or disdain for fleshly creation, you might well conceive a phobia for the good thing God had made and fall into the neurosis of **Frigidity**. Sexless marriages that end in divorce grow out of this particular vice.

- At the opposite pole from deadly **Wrath** is not holy **Patience** but masochistic **Servility**, which teaches us to let aggressors win and bullies triumph, whatever the cost to the next victim.

- **Gluttony** amounts to consuming fleshly pleasures like food or wine in the wrong quantities or the wrong way. A sane **Temperance** keeps every appetite in check by the force of reason and self-restraint— while gnostic **Insensibility** learns to see food as interchangeable nutrition units and wine as evil in itself.

- The **Greedy** have too strong an attachment to the good things that come from hard work and wise stewardship. The **Generous** love wealth in due proportion and have mastered the art of sharing it. The **Prodigal**, on the other hand, treat wealth with jaded disdain and lavishly waste it—certain that more will somehow come to them down the pike.

- **Sloth** is a sin not so much of laziness as of apathy, of the sort that can lead to despair. The **Diligent** learn how to apply themselves with sane resignation and a realist's appreciation of their limitations and weaknesses—while **Fanatics** hurl themselves headfirst into walls, torment the people who love them, and if they don't blow themselves up, they burn out and slump into . . . Sloth.

- **Vainglory** teaches people to preen themselves and be proud of nothing real, or nothing for which they deserve any credit. You can counter this vice by the starkly honest practice of **Humility**, which takes a frank account of your actual pluses and minuses. Or you can panic at the prospect you might, just *might*, be proud—and learn to rip yourself to shreds through **Scrupulosity**.

- The opposite of **Envy**—the devil's own sin, which hates the good for being good—is not the large-souled virtue of **Magnanimity** but the timid, vacuous sin called **Pusillanimity**—the kind of thing that drives a servant to bury his master's treasure in the yard.[130]

So the virtuous road, which takes proper account of our own rights and our neighbors' in any moral or political issue, is to seek the course that grants proportionate justice to all legitimate claims. That means we cannot seize on a single supposed good and bulldoze ahead, ignoring every objection.

Making a Virtue of Hysteria

But that is precisely what Progressives (including Progressive Christians) do on countless issues, from poverty reduction to crime and public safety. They identify a genuine evil, such as domestic poverty or a rising murder rate in our inner cities. They become emotionally involved in it and are rightly concerned to correct it. In the process, however, too many abandon the principle of justice, and the Golden Mean. They seize on what seems like the most obvious solution—get the government (usually the federal government) to use or expand its power to tax and coerce our fellow citizens. They rarely consider the unseen costs of their policies on other innocent citizens, and they wave aside the violation of rights entailed in heavy-handed government action.

Ignoring unseen costs, or dismissing them as unimportant, is a deeply ingrained habit on the Left. In the nineteenth century, Frédéric Bastiat summed up this political tendency as the "broken window" fallacy.[131] He imagined a politician who was concerned for the fate of unemployed glassmakers. To create more work for the glassmakers, the politician decided to break all the windows in the city. The downsides of this ought to be obvious but for too many people aren't: What of the costs to store owners, who must waste their wealth fixing windows instead of employing the money otherwise—giving other people jobs? What of the impact on glassmakers, who will come to feel entitled to state intervention on their behalf?

Every tax dollar the government seizes from citizens and dispenses would otherwise have been used some other way. The tax beneficiary's gain (minus bureaucratic cost) is the taxpayer's loss. No new wealth gets created. It just gets shifted via the government's vast Rube Goldberg system of redistribution, from one person who earned to someone who did not.

The vast explosion of federal poverty programs resulted from Progressives taking this blunt-instrument approach in the late 1960s. Never mind the numbing effects of multigenerational government dependence on the poor. For decades, conservative critics have documented how the number of illegitimate births exploded after the federal government promised full support for every child conceived out of wedlock, through non-judgmental "entitlement" programs. (See Charles Murray's *Losing Ground* and George Gilder's *Sexual Suicide*, the classics in the genre of "unintended consequences.") The result was millions of fatherless boys growing up with scant supervision and ending up in our prisons. That's the real "unseen" cost of deciding to ham-handedly solve a social problem using government force.

The "window" well-meaning liberals broke by creating the Great Society's programs was a social one—the taboo against premarital sex among poor girls, enforced by the all-too-real fear of destitution. What shattered was the inner-city family. Black out-of-wedlock birth rates skyrocketed, from 24 percent in 1965 to 64 percent in 1990, with white illegitimate births now following not far behind.[132] We've embarked on a bizarre social experiment to see whether the poorer members of our community can grow up safely without stable families or fathers. All this has taken place at a time when churches' influence has been weakening and the elite embrace of the Sexual Revolution promised "free love" without consequences.

The results are not encouraging. We see them in our prisons and in the abortion statistics, which have registered almost a million children destroyed each year since 1973.[133]

But how can we speak of the broken window fallacy after 2020 without pointing to all the glass that covered the ground in American cities, as politicians and pastors endorsed and enabled mass riots in more than a dozen U.S. cities, allegedly to advance racial justice after the death of George Floyd? How many thousands of small business owners—disproportion-ately non-white—saw outside agitators from anarchist Antifa and Marxist Black Lives Matter stir up crowds to smash their windows, help themselves to their merchandise, and menace or even try to kill anyone who resisted? Ah, but all the looting, violence, theft, destruction, and terror were justified by the claim that a single good (equity in policing) must be pursued whatever the cost. Stoking violent mobs to terrorize whole cities is considered a legitimate tactic by revolutionaries. But how could the public officials sworn to enforce the law and preserve people's rights cede control of the streets in cities such as Portland, Seattle, Minneapolis, and Kenosha to violent mobs? They made reckless promises to "defund the police," replace armed officers with social workers, and pretend that law enforcement was some species or extension of "systemic racism" that extended all the way back to 1619.

The costs of the riots were staggering. In only a two-week period in late May and early June 2020, the riots, arson, and looting caused as much as $2 billion in property damage, making them the costliest protests in U.S. history.[134] In those two weeks, at least nineteen people died, and more than seven hundred law enforcement officers were injured.[135]

The riots and the crackpot promises to defund the police led to a tsunami of crime and violence in major cities. In New York City, for example, March 2021 brought a 76 percent increase in shootings as compared with March 2020.[136] It was no accident that then-mayor Bill de Blasio abandoned his promise to defund the cops and went out seeking federal stimulus money to restore their budget. Many other Progressive politicians did the same.

Disarming the Populace and Scapegoating Dissenters

A central concern of this book is Americans' right to keep and bear arms. On the gun issue, perhaps more than any, we hear hysterical, one-sided rhetoric demanding that the state impose coercive solutions at the expense of individual rights. Whatever reassuring claims pepper their public statements (they seek "commonsense solutions" and wish to confiscate only "weapons of war"), the anti-gun lobbies are relentless in their pursuit of disarming the public, much as Australia's government did.

In that English-speaking democracy that also stands as heir to the Magna Carta, only rural hunters, after complying with elaborate bureaucratic requirements, may gain grudging permission for a few closely monitored weapons. That leaves civilians personally defenseless against violent crime, acts of terror, and any future tyrannical government. But at the heart of American liberty, according to our Founders, was an armed citizenry as the last bulwark against a possible return of tyranny. (As we will see later, the Founders sounded this theme in the debates over the ratification of the Second Amendment.) Citizens in countries like Australia must hope that their votes get honestly counted, and trust that elites will never unite sufficiently to strip them of their rights. They have no last recourse. They gave that away, and governments historically almost never give it back.

How do we know that anti-gun activists want more than they claim to? By looking at their actions. During the George Floyd riots, how did Democrat politicians and the liberal media react to reasonable exercises of Second Amendment rights on the part of honest citizens in the face of violent, destructive mobs? The Left demonized such citizens as "white supremacists" and "Christian nationalists" without presenting any evidence. Few media bothered to retract such life-ruining accusations once rigorous searches turned up zero support for them.

Of course, we've already seen the extremes to which such activists, including duly elected public prosecutors, proved willing to go. Abandon the Golden Mean as your lodestone, and it's all too easy instead to adopt the iron fist.

Pursuing the Golden Mean is the result of a craving not so much for moderation and stability as for justice. We wish to pursue a course that takes into full account all the real factors at work in a situation—instead of simply those that happen to be politically "sexy" at the moment, or popular with elites.

Think back to how completely our cultural leaders failed to do that during the George Floyd riots. America saw videotape that strongly suggested at least one police officer used excessive force while arresting a black man, ending with the citizen's death. Within days, that cop was off the force, in custody, and facing serious criminal charges. Isn't that how our system is meant to work?

Nonetheless, leftist organizers began fomenting riots, as if the policeman involved had gotten off scot-free. Professional agitators funded by sources we still don't know—nobody has investigated—flew from city to city, provoking "peaceful" daytime protests that night after night degenerated into violent, destructive riots. Mayors in city after city withheld law enforcement resources, leaving ordinary citizens completely unprotected. A section of the city of Seattle effectively seceded from the United States, declaring itself an "autonomous zone" governed by armed gangs of political thugs, like some enclave in Somalia.[137]

Clearly, accounts were imbalanced. There had been a large-scale political crime, backed by an extensive seditious conspiracy, committed against the United States. The guilty parties went unpunished, even uninvestigated. Rioters who set fire to police cars and federal courthouses walked off uncharged, emboldened. On a subconscious level, as the dubious ballots and midnight recounts of the 2020 election restored elites' vision of "normalcy" to America, our leaders in media and government knew there must be some kind of reckoning for the explosion of political violence in our country.

Compare that with what happened on January 6, 2021. A small number of pro-Trump demonstrators broke into the U.S. Capitol, thus repeating the kind of incursions into various state capitols that leftists have routinely engaged in. Dozens of other protestors walked in right past police, who removed barriers and let them waltz in. But the Democratic Party, its media allies, and federal law enforcement weren't willing to grant Trump supporters anything like the lax treatment they'd demanded for violent rioters all across the country. Instead, as if they were consciously engaged in a vast act of national scapegoating, the left treated the ludicrous spectacle of a futile election rally at the U.S. Capitol as if it were the firing on Fort Sumter or the attack on Pearl Harbor. (Prominent Progressives made direct comparisons to both events, while former president George W. Bush explicitly compared the January 6 protestors to the 9/11 suicide bombers.)[138] As the media responded hysterically, law enforcement cracked down savagely. More than a year after the event, dozens of peaceful protestors still languished in solitary confinement awaiting court dates.[139] A nakedly partisan congressional committee demanded the private records of the leading grassroots conservative activists in America. Now Trump himself and his advisors face a raft of criminal charges for even questioning the election results.

Perhaps we ought to reexamine the popular notion of "Trump Derangement Syndrome" and see it in less an intellectual than a zoological light. The dominant caste of primates in America saw a challenge to its control of vital resources and responded with primal rage, unleashing sufficient violence to restore the old dominance structure. How fitting that diplomaed Darwinists lived up to their materialistic worldview by reducing American politics to a subhuman level.

The only way to restore a truly humane politics and culture is to rediscover the habit of trying to think and act virtuously, in a balanced and rational fashion, taking account of the many real values that come into conflict in life. That means rejecting hysterical moralism and alarmism of the sort our media like to promote. It demands that we ask tough questions and refuse to take part in the witch trial atmosphere that seeks to identify, isolate, and "cancel" dissenters from fashionable causes. It demands, first and foremost, courage.

CHAPTER 7

THE NATURAL LAW IS THE ONLY BEDROCK FOR OUR LAWS

Perhaps the most fundamental question in politics is this: What is the proper source of law? Does it originate simply in the will of the powerful, imposing their wishes on the weaker? (The "powerful" might be a tribal chief, a king backed by armed warriors, or a technocratic state that claims the support of the majority of citizens, themselves swayed and led by media that the powerful control.) Clearly one must have power exercised in some form if law is to prevail at all, instead of mere disorder.

But is the source of all law, government policy, taxation, and income redistribution grounded in nothing more than that? That would leave essentially the stark assertion: *"We do these things because we can. Just try and stop us."*

If that were true, then every argument about justice, equal treatment, and individual rights would be empty rhetoric used by one group seeking power grounded in no deeper truth about existence, or human nature, or basic right and wrong. That is the bleak conclusion of philosopher Thomas Hobbes, who sees human beings as isolated atoms colliding in a godless void, seeking satisfaction of their primal urges and desperately avoiding death.

Our Real Founding Philosophy: Biblical Human Dignity

America was founded on something much richer. A few Deists worked with a large majority of Augustinian Christians in drawing up the Declaration of Independence and Constitution. But the overwhelming consensus of patriots who rallied to overthrow British power was clear. Man has a given nature, one given him by God. He has an eternal dignity, as the image of that God. Flowing from his nature and his dignity, he has "unalienable" rights that the state and his fellow citizens must respect—including and especially religious freedom, the first freedom defended in America's Bill of Rights.

How did America's Founders come to this conclusion? In the book *America on Trial*, scholar Robert Reilly explains how the very idea of human freedom grew from specific historical roots.[140] Without each of these elements, the freedom we treasure would simply be unthinkable—as in, no one would have thought of it. Those roots include:

- Ancient Greek philosophy, which judges the universe as making sense in a way that man can perceive via reason. We are not ruled by capricious gods or mindless cosmic forces.
- Jewish revelation, which taught us that a personal God made all. And he made us with minds that reflect his own. His goodness precedes his power, and we can learn about that goodness by thinking rationally about his words and deeds.
- The Christian incarnation, in which the Word became flesh in a single human person. God showed us that each individual is his image and likeness, deserving the same respect.

The synthesis of these influences, Reilly shows, laid down the roots of freedom and constitutional government. That happened not in the Enlightenment or the Renaissance but during the Middle Ages. That's where we find the first claims by Christians (like Thomas Aquinas) that persons have basic rights which no ruler may trample. Those who do are tyrants, who lose their legitimacy and deserve to be overthrown. Ironically, in many Catholic and Lutheran countries, monarchs succeeded in agglomerating absolute power—even over the Church—while in mixed, quasi-Protestant England they failed to monopolize public worship or disarm the population. So, the medieval tradition of rights-based resistance to tyranny would be passed along by Protestant settlers in America.

The idea of a higher law, with deeper roots than those imposed by any given government, is a profound one, and it has proven controversial wherever thinkers dared to suggest it. Obviously, few rulers welcome constraints on their power. Tyrants often persecute those who, as prophets, point to the ways in which unjust laws and evil practices violate fundamental Natural Law. Indeed, the recurring conflict between Natural Law prophets and pragmatic, unprincipled rulers goes all the way back to Classical Greece. As Jason Jones and I wrote in *The Race to Save Our Century*:

> Sophocles put this awareness of a transcendent law in the mouth of Antigone, who sacrifices her life to disobey King Creon's unjust edict. In the play, her brother, Polyneices, committed treason by attacking the city of Thebes, and died in battle. Creon decides to impose on Polyneices the ultimate punishment— to deny his soul rest in the underworld by refusing him proper burial. His body is left to the dogs and crows, and the death penalty is promised for anyone who dares to inter him.
>
> Antigone confronts the king, whose power is theoretically absolute, and insists that his laws are subject to an extralegal arbiter, the laws of the gods. . . . She tells Creon that she defied his decree because it's

"not a law decreed by Zeus, nor by Zeus' daughter, Justice, who rules with the gods of the Underworld. Nor do I believe that your decrees have the power to override those unwritten and immutable laws decreed by the gods."

"These are laws which were decreed neither yesterday nor today but from a time when no man saw their birth; they are eternal! How could I be afraid to disobey laws decreed by any man when I know that I'd have to answer to the gods below if I had disobeyed the laws written by the gods, after I died?"[141]

The early Christians took on Antigone's mantle when they refused the commands of the Roman state that they venerate the reigning emperor as an incarnate god and burn incense before his image. Christian dissenters against intolerant governments (both Catholic and Protestant) looked to them as exemplars when they insisted on following their consciences, not the king's.

The American Founders carried on this tradition. The next to bear the torch were the abolitionists, who insisted that man's fundamental nature, as knowable by reason, overrode evil laws and even our Constitution.

The righteous fury with which we fought World War II was fueled in part by our horror at Fascist disdain for man's natural rights. The United States insisted, against other Allies' resistance, that the Nuremberg Trials cite a "higher law" that superseded any national legislation, such as Hitler's Nuremberg Laws, and hang men for violating it. [142]

It was only logical, then, for the civil rights movement to rest not on conflict among the races but on the claims of the Natural Law. Rev. Martin Luther King Jr. cited that law in his "Letter from Birmingham Jail," writing: "How does one determine when a law is just or unjust? A just law is a man-made code that squares with the moral law, or the law of God. An unjust law is a code that is out of harmony with the moral law. To put it in the terms of St. Thomas Aquinas, an unjust law is a human law that is not rooted in eternal and natural law."[143] King claimed that Natural Law's tenets rendered null and void the local segregation laws his followers peacefully flouted.

Today the pro-life movement, and our resistance to LGBT and transgender madness, rests on Natural Law. Without it, we grope and collide blindly, exactly as Hobbes insisted. We and our opponents would equally be "ignorant armies [who] clash by night."[144]

Lesser Breeds Without the Law

How ignorant? Let's look at where our society has gone since elites dismissed Natural Law. The best way I can think of to illuminate it is in the light of a classic poem, "Recessional" by Rudyard Kipling. He wrote it as a prayer for his fellow subjects of Queen Victoria to whisper while contemplating their empire:

If, drunk with sight of power, we loose

Wild tongues that have not Thee in awe,

Such boastings as the Gentiles use,

Or lesser breeds without the Law—

Lord God of Hosts, be with us yet,

Lest we forget—lest we forget![145]

Now this is the kind of poem you can't teach in college today. Except, perhaps, as an appalling instance of crimethink. Kipling supported the British Empire and saw it as a self-sacrificial enterprise. (See his even more infamous poem, "The White Man's Burden.") And he dared, this straight white male, to speak of "lesser breeds"!

In today's climate, activists would be quick to label this an instance of "white supremacy," which is the same as "terrorism." It's all indistinguishable from Nazism, so the poet deserves to be punched. And fired from his job. Then hounded wherever he goes. And banned from social media. Maybe pummeled into the sidewalk by the triggered soy boys of Antifa.

Inconveniently, Kipling is dead. And Progressives have not quite progressed (as of this writing, check back next week!) to digging up their enemies' skeletons and dumping them into rivers. So they'll have to settle for tearing down his statues and renaming anything christened for him.

But if you bother to understand the poem, you see it was in fact a broadside *against* pride of race and nation. A sobering slap in the face to Brits and their world-bestriding hauteur. In a previous stanza the poet offered this warning:

Far-called, our navies melt away;

On dune and headland sinks the fire:

Lo, all our pomp of yesterday

Is one with Nineveh and Tyre!

Judge of the Nations, spare us yet,

Lest we forget—lest we forget!

By "lesser breeds without the Law," Kipling didn't mean blacks or Asians. The "Law" he referred to wasn't British common law but God's Law, the Natural Law he wrote on every human heart, and on the tablets of the Commandments. A law our fallen nature goads us to flout. A law the Church passed on to us, and our laws and mores reinforced, until a few decades ago.

By that exacting standard, we know who the "lesser breeds" are today, and who chooses to live "without the Law." We have met the enemy, and he is us.

Among lesser breeds without the Law:

Civilians cower as mass shooters pick them off one by one in bars or Walmarts. Our internet message boards hum with the kinked-up, bitter thoughts of young men who never had fathers pound that Law into them when they acted as bullies or brutes. Or young men whose schoolteachers disapproved of boys on general principle and so tried to drug the jumpy ones into Ritalin zombies.

Among lesser breeds without the Law:

Young people yawn as professors solemnly teach them Darwin, piously reminding them that all life is a meaningless side effect of random mutations. But hey, racism is wrong because of . . . well, because it insults our human dignity, which we derive from. . . . Well, it's wrong because it violates freedom, and you should write that down because it's gonna be on the test. Because I *said* so!

Among lesser breeds without the Law:

The wise ones remind the bitter young men: Don't get too excited about all that human dignity, kids. Because, you see, we're a plague on the planet. There are far too many of us, and we're living much too lavishly. It's wrong to have more than one or two children, and shameful to raise six or seven. Life itself might end on earth within a dozen years because we have raped the once-pristine biosphere. We'd all be better off if the world population plummeted.

Among lesser breeds without the Law:
Each new child born is seen as a parasite, sucking the life out of Gaia. Which is just another reason why abortion must be legal right up through birth."

Among lesser breeds without the Law:
Our borders, left mostly unguarded, are swarmed by entitled foreigners demanding benefits from our government that they never paid into. Or they're seeking jobs outside the law, at the expense of citizens and legal aliens, who will pay for those benefits, on penalty of imprisonment for tax evasion. Cartels of drug traffickers control who comes and goes into the country. They'll sell, or rent, children plucked off the street in Juarez for use as "Get Into America, Free" cards. Or they'll be employed as slaves on egg farms.[146] Or they'll be used as victims of American pedophiles and child pornography makers.[147]

Among lesser breeds without the Law:
Politicians collude to take down national borders. One faction does that to stuff the ballots with the cheap-bought votes of the poor, the other to stuff the bank accounts of investors in businesses that depend on cheap labor. The one thing they can agree on: Anyone who interferes with their profitable enterprise is a vicious "racist" – whatever that word even

means anymore. It's up there with "fascist" as a synonym for "doubleplusungood."

Among lesser breeds without the Law:

Aristocrats warn the commoners that we are unworthy of the liberties our forefathers deeded us. Our forebears hunted freely and wielded weapons to defend their kin and ward off tyranny. But that's not safe anymore, the new masters remind us. None of us has the self-control needed for freedom. And so we cannot be trusted. The state must control all the weapons and silence disruptive speech. Then we sheep may safely graze.

To this we have Kipling's answer:

For heathen heart that puts her trust

In reeking tube and iron shard,

All valiant dust that builds on dust,

And guarding, calls not Thee to guard,

For frantic boast and foolish word—

Thy mercy on Thy People, Lord!

By rejecting Natural Law, American elites have left our laws to rest only on the will of those elites and of unhinged activists who can weaponize the undirected anger of poorly educated mobs. The courts often reflect this elite opinion. In

2022, in the case of *Dobbs v. Jackson*, the U.S. Supreme Court finally overturned *Roe v. Wade*, which even many pro-abortion-rights liberals had conceded was a mess of a decision.[148] But plenty of conservatives had thought the Court would reverse *Roe* thirty years earlier, in *Planned Parenthood v. Casey* (1992). Hadn't President Ronald Reagan reshaped the Court with his four appointments?

Instead, a turncoat Reagan appointee, Anthony Kennedy, issued a majority opinion in *Casey* that was stunning for its nihilism, dressed up in the faux profound language of an undergrad philosophy paper. The vision of liberty that Kennedy's opinion enshrined as binding constitutional jurisprudence was a void, a hole in Being akin to the "nothingness" that the French Communist writer Jean-Paul Sartre used to describe human existence. It was numinous doubletalk, sophomoric in the literal sense of a college sophomore who read enough existentialist noodling to weaponize it for the purpose of getting "spiritual but not religious" coeds to sleep with him.

Referring to questions about the morality of killing unborn children, Kennedy wrote for the Court:

> These matters, involving the most intimate and personal choices a person may make in a lifetime, choices central to personal dignity and autonomy, are central to the liberty protected by the Fourteenth Amendment. At the heart of liberty is the right to define one's own concept of existence, of meaning, of the universe, and of the mystery of human life.

Beliefs about these matters could not define the attributes of personhood were they formed under compulsion of the State.[149]

Now, an honest originalist judge reading the Fourteenth Amendment—passed by an abolitionist Congress in the wake of the Civil War—would dismiss Kennedy's argument pretty quickly. It was clearly not the intent of the drafters or ratifiers of that amendment to legalize abortion nationwide, or to license every form of private sexual behavior. Likewise, an originalist would reject the unhinged *Bostock* decision of 2020, which pretended that the Civil Rights Act of 1965, by banning sex discrimination, had granted special protections to those who claim to be transgender. Nor can any honest person pretend that the lawmakers who passed the Civil Rights Act intended it to cover men who wished to compete in women's sports.

In his brilliant majority opinion in *Dobbs v. Jackson*, Justice Samuel Alito didn't just overturn *Roe v. Wade* and *Planned Parenthood v. Casey*. You could say he shredded them. But that wouldn't be quite right either, since no shreds even remain. Alito's careful, dispassionate scholarship—which took no position on the morality of abortion—annihilated those jerry-rigged, duct-tape-and-chewing-gum precedents.

What was most notable about the Progressive reaction to the *Dobbs* decision? It had little to do with the constitutional merits of the *Dobbs* decision or of *Roe* and *Casey*. Sure, some legal scholars tried to poke holes in Alito's arguments, but you didn't see many full-throated defenses of the two dead "super-precedents."

Instead, the Left responded with political hysteria. You heard calls to pack the Supreme Court.[150] A man traveled across the country to try to assassinate Justice Brett Kavanaugh before the justice could cast a deciding vote to overturn *Roe*.[151] The months after the *Dobbs* ruling leaked brought violent attacks and vandalism against more than eighty crisis pregnancy centers and pro-life groups.[152]

We're at the point in our national exorcism where the demon gives up making pretentious philosophical arguments and just starts howling blasphemies, spitting blood, and trying to strangle the priest.

Originalism Is Not Enough

Important as it is, judicial originalism is not enough. Americans don't feel bound by the social mores or private intentions of long-dead lawmakers, whether those of 1965, 1868, or 1787. So long as social conservatives rely solely on the original-intent argument, they might win intellectual battles, but they will lose the political war. Our society is less deferential to tradition and prescribed wisdom than ever, so they make a poor counterforce to the urgent demands of activists claiming that they are the victims of "injustice" and "discrimination," with equal moral claims to the black victims of Jim Crow laws. On the contrary, we must ground our reading of the laws our ancestors passed in the Natural Law that binds each generation and undergirded America's founding.

Legal scholar Hadley Arkes rightly calls for a "better originalism," one that relies not just on the morals that were current when a constitutional provision or law was enacted but also on what we can know by reason about man's nature, his dignity, and hence his rights.[153] That robust sense of what is "fitting" for man in light of his moral, biological, and spiritual nature is in the long run the only real restraint on the rule of blind force, fashion, and faction.

But between our effort to look at man's nature for the outline of Natural Law and popular success lies a vast Berlin Wall: the edifice of Darwinism. Charles Darwin's speculative effort to account for the "appearance of design" in nature gave nonbelievers a plausible set of arguments against our assertions of "purpose" in human nature. If the existence of the universe is a meaningless cosmic accident, and if life by some secular miracle leapt fully armored from the mud like Athena from Zeus's head, then doesn't that create the void Justice Kennedy insisted on? Shouldn't we regard life as a shapeless "mystery" unknowable by reason—where the best we can do is leave each other alone and keep pretty much any perversity we can think of "safe and legal"?

Of course, the Darwininian wall is not impenetrable. Darwin himself admitted, in candid moments of self-doubt, that natural selection can explain the survival of the fittest but not their *arrival*.[154] Moreover, Darwinians don't acknowledge the inconsistencies in their own worldview. Even though

Darwinian theory tells us that we're meaningless epiphenomena of random cosmic burps and vicious competition, somehow we also have dignity and rights, including the right to "equity." (Insert stolen premises from the Gospel worldview here.) But theology, the science that teaches us about that dignity and those rights, should curl up and die once we've taken what we wanted. The Woke folk will decide what "equality," "equity" and "justice" mean.

These are the moral reasons why we must reject the Darwinist worldview. But the scientific reasons are piling up all around us, for those who are paying attention. The Discovery Institute compiles that mounting evidence at EvolutionNews. org, and it publishes many scholarly books by scientists documenting the vast evidential gaps that have left Darwin's materialist edifice shaking in the wind.

You won't hear about them in the media, and your kids won't read them in school. It's only in "insider" scientific circles that experts wring their hands about the plummeting plausibility of materialistic, random explanations for 1) an inhabitable universe, 2) the eruption of life on earth, and 3) the emergence of man himself, complete with a consciousness capable of doing reliable, objective science.

Since Darwinist materialism is philosophically the river flowing out of Chernobyl, poisoning modern culture with nihilism (à la Anthony Kennedy's), we need to learn how to address it. No Natural Law will stand if man is the fruit of random accidents. That's why I urge you to read up on the growing body of literature exposing the holes in Darwinism.[155]

But if you want a quick introduction, start with . . . Sonny Bono.

You see, decades before he became a congressman, Bono met and fell in love with Cher when she was only sixteen. And he had to break the news to her: Mount Rushmore is not a natural formation.[156]

The story makes Cher sound foolish, right? After all, how could the random forces of nature have formed precise portraits of four human beings? Not just any humans, but American politicians. And not just any politicians, but four men who became key U.S. presidents. Why didn't the wind and rain slowly carve into the granite the faces of, say, James Buchanan, Warren Harding, William Henry Harrison, and William Jefferson Clinton?

But maybe we should cut Cher some slack. The idea of "natural erosion"—of blind chance and mindless forces carving out four prominent presidents over millions of years—is no less suspect than the concept of natural selection. "Random chance" is far less powerful than pop Darwinism has led most people to believe. That became increasingly clear to scientists in the wake of the discovery of DNA, the alphabet that encodes the elaborate information found in the tiniest, most primitive cell.[157] Mathematicians in the late 1960s pointed out that DNA was a code, analogous to computer code. And in the experience of computer programmers, random combinations of letters never generate functional programs. Random mistakes in coding (analogous to mutations) never result in better programs. They just stop the programs from working, as virtually all large-scale genetic mutations, it turns out in the lab, result in nonviable offspring, not new and improved Darwinian leaps toward better "fitness."

If anything, the odds are much better that nature could have carved out Mount Rushmore on its own than that any of the following things happened randomly (at least not in the amount of time that has elapsed in the history of the universe):

- Organic chemicals combined to form the immensely complex and fragile structures of enzymes and proteins. *(Imagine alphabet soup randomly combining to form sentences. And then the recipe for alphabet soup.)*
- Those enzymes combined and learned to cooperate to form the tiny biocomputer facility we call a cell. *(The alphabet soup forms a Help Wanted ad for a chef to come cook more soup.)*
- Such cells differentiated and learned to work together to form higher organisms. *(The alphabet soup writes the chef's autobiography.)*
- The cells in those organisms underwent major mutations to form whole new physical structures of new species that weren't unviable mutants but better-adapted organisms. In decades of lab research on microorganisms, scientists have found so far zero mutations like that. *(The alphabet soup forms a series of cookbooks. It lists the chef as the author.)*

- The same process of natural selection and random mutations happened often enough, and turned out well enough, to explain how infinitesimal microorganisms "evolved" into plants, then animals, then humans. *(The alphabet soup develops into a variety of ethnic cuisines, from Jamaican to Japanese.)*

No Natural Law isn't the superstition, generated by wishful thinking on the part of clever people who seek justifications for what they want to believe. That's how we should think of Justice Kennedy and his worldview.

It's equally important to recognize that Kennedy's nihilist version of liberty was absent among the Founders. Not one of them believed it, not even the Deist Thomas Jefferson or the skeptic Ethan Allen. The political theorist Thomas G. West has documented the extent to which our Founders believed in Natural Law or relied on other philosophical grounds for asserting the colonists' political rights.[158] West lays out three sets of grounds on which liberty might be premised. Some Founders believed in one or two; others, in all three:

The God of Nature: The United States wasn't founded as a legally Christian nation. Which is just as well. Nations with overtly Christian monarchies today include Great Britain, Spain, and Sweden. But almost all of our Founders counted on America's thriving Christian culture and institutions to furnish the moral capital that kept liberty from becoming license. Moreover, many Founders cited God as the source of our wisdom insofar as his laws could be known by human reason. In other words, they believed in Natural Law. Nearly every major Founder, including even the Deists, cited this as one of the grounds for natural rights. It is the most philosophically consistent, robust, and defensible ground for discerning and asserting human rights.

The Moral Sense: Many Founders also cited this as a reason to offer men liberty and treat them as equals. It was here that the seeds of destruction for slavery were planted. John Adams, Benjamin Rush, and Thomas Jefferson were eloquent on this subject. So was John Locke. We know by looking in our hearts that we have no right to be tyrants over our fellow man. Likewise, we feel deep resentment at the thought of being tyrannized. Unfortunately, the subjective element at the heart of this rationale for freedom makes it less reliable as a philosophical guide. It is likely to shift with the times and be subject to manipulation by elites—who in one decade might favor eugenic "improvement" of the species, and in another might invent incoherent claims like those asserted by the transgender movement. Only a rationally grounded, systematic method of understanding human nature such as Natural Law can anchor timeless principles against the storms and tides of ideology.

The Natural Fitness of Things: This ground for American liberty was the most popular, West claims. It didn't rely on acceptance of God's existence or on debatable claims about the verdict of human conscience. It simply pointed to indisputable facts: No men were clearly superior to others. None were fitted by nature to take the rights of others and govern adults as if they were lifelong children or herds of cattle. Again, like the "moral sense," this rationale for liberty lacks a firm philosophical foundation and is subject to shifting opinion. But most of the political arguments we make in everyday life typically choose this ground over which to fight: What seems "fair" to people based on their current, likely inchoate sense of "how the world is."

It is our task to help people ground their sense of what "is" and "ought to be" not on shifting sand but on the solid rock of Natural Law.

CHAPTER 8

BIBLICAL HUMAN
DIGNITY AND THE RIGHT
TO SELF-DEFENSE

The term "Natural Law, as we have seen, refers to what we are able to know is right and wrong via reason alone, by reflecting on man's nature and existence as a creature of God, without necessary reference to any specific church tradition, or national customs and mores. Natural Law describes what is proper to *man as such*, regardless of race, sex, creed, or country. In practical terms, it lays out the extent and implications of human dignity, and how that translates into moral claims and political rights we must demand that the government defend.

Countless Christians have made the case against the evil of abortion based on Natural Law and human dignity. We should all be deeply grateful to the thinkers, activists, volunteers, and political fighters of the pro-life movement. The social revolution of the 1960s and '70s flattened most obstacles in its path, leaving little resistance. How many people today still resist the demands of feminism, the LGBT syndicate, or even the multiculturalist movement? They are few and far between, and mostly banned or canceled. But on the abortion issue, doughty bands first of Catholic laymen, then Catholic clergy, then later evangelical Christians and other people of principle kept this issue alive for five decades—this in the face of massive cultural pressure, biased courts' dishonest decisions, and the initial indifference of even the Republican Party.

But here I'd like to apply Natural Law reasoning about the implications of human dignity to a topic where I haven't seen it often employed: the right to keep and bear arms. As the last section of this book will document, the Christian vision of the human person and his rights is the direct, historical origin of self-defense rights in the English-speaking world (where they still survive). But that link has decayed. Even fervent Christians who support our self-defense rights rarely ground their case in Natural Law arguments, much less biblical precedent and Christian tradition. They should, and here I will.

What is the most basic human right in a fallen, violent world?

It must be that of self-defense against violence. Whether some aggressor aims at killing us, committing some grievous harm such as rape, or seizing our labor and its fruits, we feel intuitively that we as persons have the right to defend ourselves and our family members. You might say that this claim arises from our animal nature, and this is true. As embodied spirits, we hearken to the call of the flesh at dinnertime, when "nature calls," and when we decide to marry.

But man is something more. Few dogmatic Darwinian materialists will wave off blatant racism or casual rape as "ordinary primate behavior," although of course it is. We don't really think of the antelope as having the "right" to flee from the lion. Nor do we watch nature documentaries and think of the lion as violating the antelope's "rights." We don't look at termite colonies and consider that the workers are "oppressed" by the pampered queen. Nor do we look at our putative evolutionary cousins, the apes, and tut-tut at them for adultery, cannibalism or incest. Scientists rightly dismiss such reactions as examples of "anthropomorphism." There's something about human nature that evokes a different kind of reaction, which we rightly call "moral."

Yet we are not angels. Even the deeply mystical St. Francis of Assisi, for all his asceticism, embraced his physicality, using the affectionate term "Brother Ass" for his body. It might be stubborn and in need of regular discipline by the spirit, but his body was still his "brother," not his enemy or his cage. The ancient Gnostics, who infiltrated Christian churches, disagreed. They insisted that the body was the cage of the spirit, that its claims were completely opposite and were made by a lesser or even an evil god.

Their modern descendants, the Transhumanists, agree. They hope that our consciousness can be decoupled from our fragile, mortal frames and "uploaded" onto some more durable hardware of silicon and plastic. But those of us who reject both Gnostic pessimism and Transhumanist fantasies know better than to grasp at ethical systems that don't take account of the flesh and its needs.

We live in a "middle realm" or "middle earth"—the term the Anglo-Saxons coined for the realm of ordinary, mortal life. We are the "crown of creation," a "little lower than the angels." We speculate and theorize, meditate and pray, unfurl the secrets of mathematics and physics, but to do all that we must live. In bodies.

What Does the History of Slavery Prove?

That fact connects with the ugly cognitive dissonance we experience when we remember that many of our Founders were slave owners. Slaves as legal chattel had no final claim on their own bodies and labor, no recognized right of self-defense, no right to legal marriage or custody of their children. The attack that slavery constituted on their basic human rights was bodily. The law said that they could be whipped. They'd have to watch helplessly as their wives or daughters were raped.

The fundamental horror of slavery offers potent weapons to those who distrust or even reject the American system of ordered liberty. Yes, America was settled, and the United States founded, while the evil of slavery was accepted as a fact of life in almost every corner of the world, as it had been for most of human history. Does this vitiate every advance that Americans made toward human progress? Does it justify rejecting the documents produced and rights defended by imperfect men, who hadn't outpaced the world enough to outlaw slavery, too? The activists who created the 1619 Project seem to think so. That's why they twisted the documents and fudged the facts to make the entire movement of resistance to British rule in America seem like a conspiracy in defense of slavery. Better, more honest scholars have doggedly fought to correct them.[159]

Slavery was an intolerable evil—a denial of the very human dignity that the Bible affirmed and the American Founding sought to defend. Can we really hearken to Founding Fathers who owned slaves and condoned the institution? Can we listen to theologians who made allowances for it?

The answer is yes, but a qualified one. Clinging firmly to the deeper understanding of human dignity that the Christian-driven abolitionist movement insisted on, we take what is of value and leave aside the errors. Yes, we are willing to say that we know better, on this issue, than Church Fathers and popes, statesmen and philosophers, whose times taught them to wink at such an evil.

Likewise, we must be willing to confront churchmen today who have blinded themselves to the human person's right to direct, personal self-defense against crime and to the citizenry's collective right to defend itself against tyranny. My friend Jason Scott Jones, a human rights activist, responded to the U.S. Catholic bishops' embrace of the "public health" and "gun violence" language that the contemporary left promotes. Writing in the influential Catholic magazine *Legatus*, Jones recalled the basic moral issue that these bishops (like so many modern churchmen) ignore—the fundamental rights of the person. He wrote:

On the issue of gun rights and gun control, we are speaking of perhaps the most basic human right imaginable: the right to defend yourself and your family against an immediate threat of violence— either against your person or your hard-earned property. The primary function of the state is more effectively to guard our lives, liberties and property from aggression, coercion and theft.

But the state cannot be everywhere, nor would we want it to be. Given that, there will always be situations where citizens must defend themselves and their families against immediate threats from criminals. That is their inalienable right, and for the state to deprive them of that right would be intrinsically evil. No situation justifies doing what is intrinsically evil. Therefore, no argument of public policy, no appeal to some "seamless garment" or sentimentalized version of Christian non-violence, could ever justify preventing citizens from protecting themselves from violence. . . .

In many American cities, violent crime is a constant threat to citizens' well-being—not only to their safety and that of their children, but to the fruits of their hard work. The home, the car, the possessions that a member of the working poor has managed to accumulate might have taken them many years to acquire and could prove impossible to replace. But short of full-on surveillance, there is no way for the state to provide such citizens adequate protection. So these citizens must be allowed to arm themselves in a proportionate manner.

The laws governing self-defense should rightly center first and foremost on the absolute right of each human being, the image of God, to protect himself and his family—not on the calculations of distant bureaucrats or the wistful imaginings of high-minded idealists.[160]

It helps to illustrate such abstractions with facts. Unfortunately, scholars and public officials cannot agree on the best methodology to obtain reliable figures on the number of defensive gun uses (which include everything from brandishing one's weapon to scare off a criminal, to shooting a violent offender). The highest scholarly estimate, of between 2.2 million and 2.5 million such uses each year, comes from Florida State University criminologists Gary Kleck and Marc Gertz.[161] Gun prohibitionists dispute these numbers, claiming that thousands of respondents to the survey were lying to researchers. The lowest estimate of such defensive gun uses is 116,000 annual incidents. But the methodology that generated that number is also controversial, as Brian Doherty observed in *Reason* magazine.[162]

The most recent study—and the most comprehensive ever conducted—was led by Professor William English of Georgetown University. His 2021 National Firearms Survey found that "25.3 million adult Americans have used a gun in self-defense," meaning that "there are approximately 1.67 million defensive uses of firearms per year." The report added, "In most cases (81.9%) the gun is not fired." That is, simply showing the weapon proved sufficient to deter a criminal or criminals (since more than half of all incidents involve more than one assailant).[163]

Since the social science here is unsettled and our goal is to advance an argument, let's pretend that we believe the lowest number. As it happens, 116,000 is also the number of Americans who die of Alzheimer's disease each year, which makes it the sixth-leading cause of death in the country.[164] If we don't consider that a trivial number when reflecting on Alzheimer's, neither should we here. Using the lowest plausible number, every year at least as many Americans preserve their lives, families, homes, and property from violence as die of Alzheimer's.

Opponents of private firearms ownership for self-defense, those who would restrict that right so narrowly that it would essentially allow only for hunting, want to deprive Americans of the right to resist violence. They want to subject them to the traumatic, life-changing experience of being helpless in the face of aggression. They want to take away the medicine that our Founders prescribed for that evil, just as surely as someone suppressing a life-saving treatment for Alzheimer's.

Furthermore, violent crime's impact on non-white and poorer Americans is vastly disproportionate, given the disparate crime rates in such communities.[165] So suppressing private firearms use for self-defense would actually be more analogous to . . . suppressing a treatment for sickle-cell anemia. All this in the pursuit of the utopian hope that punishing law-abiding gun owners will someday—probably not in our lifetimes—result in a virtually gun-free society.

Is the government's seizure of basic human rights moral? Is it right? That's the question to pose to liberal pastors and those who heed them.

But Progressives won't follow such logic, for a wide array of reasons. In part, they have wedded themselves (as we saw in previous chapters) to a collectivist vision of man better suited not to mammals but to "eusocial" (hive) insects such as bees and termites. Who would cavil that a drone's rights are being violated when the queen, after mating, sends worker bees to expel the now useless drone and leave him to starve? That really is the subconscious model Progressives have adopted toward U.S. citizens, which emerges most fully in daylight when the issue is self-defense and guns.

For proof of that, recall where we began this book: with the left's treatment of Jake Gardner and Kyle Rittenhouse.

Nor are their cases isolated incidents. Do you remember Mark and Patricia McCloskey? In 2020, George Floyd protestors descended on the McCloskeys' St. Louis neighborhood. The couple stood outside their home holding guns, fearing that the protestors would harm them or damage their property. The McCloskeys never fired a shot. Nevertheless, the St. Louis prosecutor charged them with a felony, "unlawful use of a gun."[166] Eventually, the McCloskeys had to plead guilty to misdemeanors and pay a fine. Missouri's governor later pardoned them. But the pardon came after well over a year of attacks from the Left, not to mention the considerable costs (financial and emotional) of court battles. The couple, both attorneys, were stripped of their licenses to practice law.[167]

Another factor at work is that Progressives don't take property rights seriously as human rights. But, of course, property rights are human rights: human beings are the only creatures on earth that hold or recognize property. Decades of crass Marxist sneering at such rights in schools and colleges have eroded the healthy respect that Americans once had for what Richard Weaver called "the last metaphysical right."[168] So let's consider property rights in the context of guns, violence, crime, and the Christian view of the person.

No Lives Matter

"Black Lives Matter." What a brilliant piece of marketing that organizational label turned out to be, weaponizing a perfectly legitimate biblical sentiment in service of a Marxist sect of street thugs and corporate shakedown experts. In a 2015 interview, Black Lives Matter leader Patrisse Cullors said that she and co-founder Alicia Garza were "trained Marxists."[169] Several years later, reports emerged that this "Marxist" had spent more than $3.2 million to buy up four high-end homes.[170] By any worldly measure, that's success.

Did the organization actually succeed in increasing the reverence for black Americans' lives, though? Not if you measure crime statistics in major cities. The rate of homicides with black victims increased 53% since the protests after the death of George Floyd.[171]

Beyond the predictable practical impact on poor people's lives of crippling the police, what philosophical effect did the unhinged assault on criminal justice have?

We can all agree with the words, if not with the race hustlers who adopted them as a trademark. The lives of black people, who are equally images of God for whom Jesus died, are sacred. And sacred things matter.

Every person of every race, regardless of wealth, privilege, ability, age, sinfulness, or any other factor, has a unique value in God's eyes. While his life, like yours and mine, is fleeting, his soul is immortal. That's what really matters. As C. S. Lewis wrote in *The Weight of Glory*, if we could see the eternal fate of every person around us—endless glory with God or eternal punishment—we couldn't get through the day. We'd be either awestruck with glory or paralyzed by horror.

All that is bedrock Christian dogma. It also happens, not by coincidence, to be the core fact on which American politics were founded. We have "unalienable" rights only because "our Creator" "endowed" us with them. They didn't grow out of the ground or fall from space. The very idea that each person carries a sacred nimbus of rights by virtue of his humanity is not something of earth. It's transcendent.

The Aztecs didn't believe that, and neither did the Confucians. Nor did the Romans, Greeks, or any other pagans. Rebels against the Bible, from Revolutionary France to Nazi Germany and Soviet Russia, strenuously denied it. Each of those pagan, post-Christian, and anti-Christian regimes carved out huge exceptions, drawing up long lists of people whose lives by their very nature (their race, or class, or religion) weren't sacred but cheap.

The sanctity of life is the proposition on which America is built. Every liberty we cling to, each institution we value, flows from that assertion. That's why slavery stuck like a bone in our forefathers' throats. It's why abortion will make our descendants ashamed of us.

There is no other stable basis for human dignity.

Life Is Too Sacred for Pacifism to Be True

Following biblical truths, we recognize that every life is unique and precious. Does that mean, at the policy level, the highest good is avoiding death at any cost?

Actually, no. If that were true, then we'd never fight any wars. We'd always decide that the price in human lives was just too high. So, we'd let bullies and tyrants (who think life is cheap) run the world. If Churchill had been a pacifist, there would have been death camps in Britain.

God didn't tell the Jews to embrace nonviolence in the Old Testament, and Jesus never endorsed it in the New. He never told soldiers to quit the Roman army as the price of following him. He did tell us to accept personal slights (like a slap on the cheek) rather than escalate to dueling, but that's as close to pacifism as Jesus ever got. He didn't come to earth to contradict his Father, who'd told the Jews to fight in self-defense against—and sometimes even to conquer—truly evil regimes built on child sacrifice.

If extending every single life as long as possible were the goal, our speed limits would have to be set at 10 miles per hour, and we'd all drive rubber cars while wearing helmets. Mountain climbing, NASCAR, football, and other dangerous sports would be illegal. We'd have no death penalty, not even for murder. But we'd also have a hard time enforcing the law in the first place. No cops would carry guns.

Are you seeing the potential for total insanity here? Nobody really believes that life extension is of infinite value. Nobody really believes that we should starve the arts, education, entertainment, and every other endeavor of funds, just to spend the money on health and nutrition. Or that we should give up our freedom and let the government force us to exercise for two hours daily, just to extend our lives. Or dictate that we eat only healthy foods, in pre-measured portions. The public health dictatorship imposed in the name of COVID did make strides toward modeling Western public life on North Korea's, but we've seen the backlash.

We do want cops to use force when necessary to stop aggressors, thieves, and terrorists. This holds true not only when lives are at stake but even when property is threatened. That's why the guards at the Vatican have guns and would use them if someone insisted on spraying the Sistine Chapel ceiling with red paint. Would that be an un-Christian decision, to have Swiss Guard snipers take out a vandal attacking that timeless art?

Absolutely not. Swiss Guards using force to defend timeless art, or a shop owner using force to defend his business, is good and right and Christian.

Think about it. What are the paintings on the Sistine Ceiling but the concrete result of an artist's life? The countless hours he poured into that work . . . they were his life. If some looter destroys it, what is he doing but stealing all those years from Michelangelo? He's in effect going back in time and murdering the man.

On a more everyday level, think of some guy in Kenosha, Wisconsin, who spent forty years working in his family's convenience store, building up a livelihood. If a bunch of rioters barge in and burn the place, they've turned all those hours into slave labor. They've made him a slave. And slaves have the right to rebel, to fight back, to resist using whatever force is necessary against those who would put them in chains.

When looters attack a shopping center, they aren't "precious human lives" who outweigh mere "bricks and mortar." They are criminals using force to try to enslave other human beings. So we ought to resist them using proportionate force. Ideally, police would do that.

The truth is, the lives of the innocent *matter more* than the lives of the guilty. The lives people have built, the businesses they've constructed by the sweat of their brows over thousands of hours, matter more than the self-indulgent whims of angry looters. When thugs initiate violence, they forfeit their right to peace. Extending their lives matters less than keeping the peace and protecting the innocent.

What happens when a government turns the streets over to rioters and stands down the police, abandoning the citizens and the law? It's abolishing democracy and making street gangs sovereign. It's making Antifa or Black Lives Matter into the state.

At that point, citizens have the right, even the duty, to step up and fight. As the brave, rash Kyle Rittenhouse did, God bless him.

PART III

WHY THE RIGHT TO BEAR ARMS IS CENTRAL TO HUMAN DIGNITY AND FREEDOM

CHAPTER 9

FROM THE TORAH TO THE CONVERSION OF CONSTANTINE

I s the Second Amendment of the U.S. Constitution just a historical quirk, as visiting foreigners from other English-speaking democracies—which don't guarantee citizens' gun rights—might observe? Is it an ugly anomaly, an illiberal blot on our otherwise admirable Bill of Rights, as U.S. Progressives seem to assume? Given how important this amendment is to the preservation of our other liberties, we could argue that gun rights are a natural and fitting inference from the premises of a free and popular government. Their absence in other countries' constitutions endangers citizens' other basic rights. In fact, I believe that.

But the right of private citizens to retain arms roughly equivalent to the rights of a nation's soldiers is not necessarily a logical conclusion. It didn't seem essential to the advocates of independence in Canada, Australia, India, or other ex-British colonies. Other nations have produced great classically liberal thinkers. Not all of them have focused on the right to keep and bear arms as crucial to the preservation of other rights. There are other means of restraining the privileges of governments over their citizens. Separation of powers is one. Drawing on Montesquieu's work, James Madison and other American Founders built that separation into the very structure of U.S. government. The idea of positing an armed citizenry as the final guarantor of all these other liberties, and enshrining the means of mass popular resistance in the Constitution itself—that was a distinctly American idea. It's one of the distinguishing marks of our culture, and should be a source of national pride.

Indeed, liberty is much more deeply rooted and less fragile in America in part because the Second Amendment protects the power to resist. The understanding that resistance to mass oppression is still possible here operates (partly subconsciously) to restrain the fantasies of aspiring tyrants and stiffen the courage of independent-minded citizens. At the height of the COVID panic, there was no question of locking unvaccinated Americans in their homes (as happened in Austria)[172] or in quarantine camps (as happened in Australia).[173] Abuses of religious freedom and parental rights that occur regularly in Canada still seem unthinkable in most parts of America. Why?

On some visceral level, our own social engineers realize that the people still have teeth.

The Fruit of Happy Accidents . . . or Providence

The centrality of gun rights to liberty in America is in some ways the fruit of a series of contingent historical events—happy accidents, one might call them. These events in the political and religious history of the English people, then the Anglo-American colonists, cemented the use of private firearms and citizen militias, demonstrating their unique power to restrain governments from abusing citizens' basic rights.

In other words, the school of experience taught lessons that abstract thinkers might otherwise never have happened upon. That in turn enriched the theoretical resources of philosophical thinkers, providing them with solid, practical proofs resolving otherwise debatable questions. If we can look to the repeated experience of our ancestors in solving crucial problems, we can summon precedent along with abstract argument. And when both those elements support our traditions, we ought to continue practicing those traditions, barring overwhelming reasons to suspend them.

Ordered liberty is possible only where the culture widely accepts a "high" view of human dignity, of man as the intentional creation and earthly image of a rational, loving God. Man so conceived is the bearer of extensive rights and the subject of equally extensive responsibilities, which are well described in the Declaration of Independence and well protected in the U.S. Constitution (rightly interpreted according to its authors' original intent).

This book has explored Natural Law precisely because a proper view of human dignity proves so important to understanding the nature of those rights and responsibilities. To resolve disputes about our rights, we must first study the text of our founding documents in their historical and religious context. But when such study cannot settle the disputes, we ought to examine the human person in the light of Natural Law. This tradition of reflection on human flourishing began with Aristotle, deepened in the Middle Ages, and continued into the generation of the American Founders. Natural Law sees intentionality and purpose in the structure of the world, in our bodies, and in the basic institutions of society. We are not electrons colliding in the void, revolving around the nucleus of an all-powerful state.

Those who attempt to smuggle in reductionist accounts of mankind—as the trousered ape, in the view of Darwin and Marx, or as the Promethean rebel against God, in the view of the Marquis de Sade and the Jacobins—are undermining freedom. Intentionally or not, they are crafting rationales for the tyrannical domination of some men by other men.

The same cynical view of man that which makes psychological excuses for violent criminals of a fetishized ethnic minority will pathologize or criminalize political dissent on the part of honest citizens. Hence, the violent felons confronted by beleaguered police in major cities appear as victims of "systemic racism." But the peaceful protestors still locked in solitary after January 6, 2020 get painted as akin to al Qaeda terrorists. Hate speech aimed at police gets excused as "protest," while fact-based dissents from the shifting NIH) party line on COVID-19 suffer censorship as "dangerous" or "harmful" "misinformation." "Kill Whitey" passes muster, but "Try Ivermectin" gets you banned for life.

The quirks and accidents of history helped unearth and make fully visible the genuine rights of man as God made him. To defend our particular American liberties—and especially the right to self-defense against both individual violence and state-sponsored tyranny—we'll need to know at least in outline the course of that historical discovery, as America's English settlers and later the American Founders saw it. That history shows why the U.S. Constitution protects our God-given rights—for the moment, anyway.

It All Starts with the Hebrew Bible

As we have seen, one of the most dangerous temptations for Christians is to bracket the whole Old Testament, to act as if Jesus had come to abolish the Law, reveal a totally new face of God, or even (in effect) proclaim a new God with different attributes from the Jewish one. That's what the early Church uber-heretic Marcion taught, openly and proudly. Today's Progressive Christians too often imitate him, waving off inconvenient Old Testament passages as if they weren't still Holy Writ. We see this happen most often with prohibitions of illicit sexual acts, especially among LGBTQMYNAMEISLEGION activists.

Both to understand our country's founding culture and to discover the theological truths it encoded in law, we must understand the Jewish tradition of thinking about self-defense. Happily, the legal scholar David Kopel has delved into this question in his book *The Morality of Self-Defense and Military Action: The Judeo-Christian Tradition.*[174] His findings shed light on the development of the Second Amendment.

Kopel points both to the letter of Scripture and to the subsequent Jewish traditions of interpreting and applying it. The passage he cites is directly relevant to the defensive use of firearms in foiling crimes today. It's equally relevant to the mindset of Bible-reading Puritans who formed the most influential political communities in Colonial America. Those Puritans were more steeped in the Old Testament than most Christians, seeing themselves as latter-day heirs of the nation of Israel. They were also afraid of crime, Indian raids, and attacks by the neighboring French settlers in Canada.

Exodus 22:2 teaches: "If a thief is found breaking in, and is struck so that he dies, there shall be no bloodguilt for him; but if the sun has risen upon him, there shall be bloodguilt for him."

As Kopel explains, both the Hellenistic Jewish scholar Philo and the Babylonian Talmud offered rational accounts of the standard here imposed. We may use force to defend our private property from robbers. But that force ought to be restrained, not seeking the death of the offender. That changes if the attack occurs at night—at which point deadly force becomes legitimate.

Why? The Jewish thinkers realized that a nighttime intrusion into the family home was a greater offense, one that threatened the bodily safety of women and children in the vulnerable condition of being undressed and likely asleep. A night attack also made help from neighbors in apprehending the thief unlikely.

Kopel connects ordinary theft to the organized theft and coercion proper to tyrannical governments:

> Like the Romans, Philo viewed all forms of theft as merely variations on a single type of attack on society: as assault on the right of ownership of private property. Thus a petty thief was no different in principle from a tyrant who stole the resources of his nation, or a nation that plundered another nation. Later, Christian theologian Augustine of Hippo (354–430 CE) made a similar point, asking, "If justice be taken away, what are governments but great bands of robbers?"[175]

These are ideas worth chewing on as we watch governments in blue cities such as San Francisco and New York City effectively decriminalize the theft of property from stores. Such suspensions of the most basic principles of common law are more than just sops to "community leaders" and race-hustling activists. They are rejections of biblical, classical, and Natural

Law precepts, which hold that private property is the foundation of freedom and peaceful cooperation among human beings. Political leaders who reject private property in principle will prove to be tyrants in practice.

And indeed they have. The architects of the Terror in Revolutionary France combined mass murder with mass theft. They confiscated vast properties that pious laymen had willingly given the Church, under the euphemism of "secularization." Those farms and vineyards—often reclaimed from wilderness and carefully tended by monks for centuries—the Jacobins sold to their cronies at bargain prices. Then they used the revenues to fund their wars of "liberation" against France's neighbors. (In this, the revolutionaries were merely following the playbook of England's King Henry VIII.)[176]

Subsequent tyrannical regimes in Russia, Mexico, and Spain followed suit—also confiscating large estates without compensation. Those thefts they labeled "land reform."

In a grotesque imitation, the National Socialists in Germany seized property from Jews. They stole everything from newspapers and homes to eyeglasses and pocket watches. The euphemism employed for simple theft in this case? An adaptation of the old Jacobin usage: "Aryanization."[177]

Misreading Romans 13

The most common Christian arguments against resisting tyranny stem from misreadings of a key passage in St. Paul's letter to the Romans. This was the favorite passage of Lutheran pastors in Hitler's Germany when they wished to excuse themselves from speaking out against Nazi abuses—back when the German church might still have helped to stop them.[178] Here is the relevant section in full:

> Let every person be subject to the governing authorities. For there is no authority except from God, and those that exist have been instituted by God. Therefore he who resists the authorities resists what God has appointed, and those who resist will incur judgment. For rulers are not a terror to good conduct, but to bad. Would you have no fear of him who is in authority? Then do what is good, and you will receive his approval, for he is God's servant for your good. But if you do wrong, be afraid, for he does not bear the sword in vain; he is the servant of God to execute his wrath on the wrongdoer. Therefore one must be subject, not only to avoid God's wrath but also for the sake of conscience. For the same reason you also pay taxes, for the authorities are ministers of God, attending to this very thing. Pay all of them their dues, taxes to whom taxes are due, revenue to whom revenue is due, respect to whom respect is due, honor to whom honor is due. (Romans 13:1–7)

A wrong reading of this passage would imply that Holy Scripture condemned in advance:

- Christian revolts against Muslim oppression—such as the seizure of girls for sex slavery, and boys for forced conversion and military service.
- Armed resistance to religious persecution, such as Calvinists suffered in France and Catholics in Ireland.
- Slave revolts, such as happened in Haiti.
- The establishment of American independence from Britain.
- The establishment of Irish independence from Britain.
- The French resistance to the legally constituted Vichy regime.
- The use of force against Great Britain to establish the State of Israel.

If your reading of a Bible verse leads to outrageous consequences that violate Natural Law or vitiate the Old Testament, or that seem to condemn the behavior of many saints . . . then you are indeed reading it wrong.

I have too much reverence for St. Paul's human wisdom, beside the inspiration of Scripture, to take this prudent piece of advice and run with it over the Gadarene slope into the sea. That is what many Christians have done over the centuries— for instance, by teaching that slavery was legal and hence must be accepted, or by telling their congregations to be "good Germans" and obey the Nazis.

St. Paul was writing to a group of underground Christians living in an absolute monarchy dressed up like a republic. In the

Rome of his day, wealthy senators could be falsely denounced for treason and then summarily executed, with their estates seized for the state. He'd seen Jewish Zealots crucified for rebelling against the Romans. He knew that a third or more of that city's population were slaves. Furthermore, Paul was concerned to make clear to his readers that the Church was not a political movement seeking power. Instead, it was a family concerned with preaching the Gospel and offering sacraments, such as Baptism.

Paul did wish to rebuke those tempted to anarchism or antinomianism, who thought that the Kingdom of Christ dethroned all earthly authority and laws. He taught that it is good for men to live in organized societies, where legitimate rulers protected order and punished crimes. Some Christian thinkers have argued that the Fall is the only reason men need to have governments. Thomas Aquinas disagreed, asserting that even unfallen men would still need a single authority to organize and rule them.

Many early Christians were tempted to absolute pacifism— rejection of military and even police use of force. Later on, many others would be drawn to political quietism—refusal to resist evil laws or unjust authorities.

How did Christians get from that passage in Romans above to affirming, with the Continental Congress:

When in the Course of human events, it becomes necessary for one people to dissolve the political bands which have connected them with another, and to assume among the powers of the earth, the separate and equal station to which the Laws of Nature and of Nature's God entitle them, a decent respect to the opinions of mankind requires that they should declare the causes which impel them to the separation.

The answer is . . . very gradually, through a series of crises that forced people to think more deeply about what God did and didn't mean by including such a passage in Scripture. And to think that through in light of what else was to be found in both Old and New Testaments, and in situations that St. Paul did not envision.

The Roots of Christian Resistance to Tyranny

The letter to the Romans was written long before the Roman Empire began its widespread, systematic persecution of Christians. Nero's attacks on the Roman Christian community might have seemed at the time a one-off. Or the perversity of a ruler given to other atrocities. But future emperors would emulate Nero in believing the worst whispered slanders about Christians as secret cannibals, anarchists, and enemies of Rome.

The inherent flaws would emerge in an autocratic system built on widespread slavery and imperialistic conquest, with no reliable system for choosing new emperors. The original natural virtues that had made Roman dominance possible receded into the past.

Instead of citizen armies who'd leave off ploughing for a season to defend a Republic, Rome developed a vast mercenary army to occupy the sprawling territories conquered by ambitious generals like Caesar and Pompey, and to keep loot flowing to the Eternal City. Soon the ranks were filled with foreign recruits. The troops of various legions gave their loyalty to commanders who rewarded them financially instead of to the abstraction that was Rome. That meant that every time an emperor died, or politically faltered, civil war was a very real prospect. The army became a kind of nation unto itself, with less and less connection to civilian politics or local communities.[179]

And Christians proved a useful scapegoat, again and again, for emperors looking for someone to blame for the empire's declining fortunes. At the same time, the effort to shore up the emperors' authority included formal "divinization" by the Senate. As early as the reign of the first emperor, Augustus, there were shrines where his great-uncle Julius was worshiped as a god. The cult of the divine emperor quickly expanded to include still-living rulers, like the fourth emperor, Claudius. And over the course of decades, paying divine honors ceased to be voluntary; emperors imposed it as a test of political loyalty.

Christians realized that worshiping a living man as a god was not covered by St. Paul's dictates in Romans. The First Commandment forbade it. The example of the Maccabees suggested that God preferred outright rebellion to participation in paganism. But pacifist scruples persisted, and in any case, Christians recognized the utter impossibility of overthrowing the Romans. These factors combined to encourage among Christians a veneration for martyrdom. Jesus called us to follow him and take up our crosses. Perhaps the purest witness to Christian faith was to literally die on one, as St. Peter would. Except for St. John, every one of the eleven faithful Apostles would die as martyrs (some to the Romans, some to the Pharisees).

Countless Roman women, converted to Christianity, refused pagan marriages and instead vowed virginity. Many were executed on the authority of the fathers whom they'd defied. They were venerated by the Church, and that fact helped cement for the first time in the West the principle that women's free consent was essential to marriage.

Many of the early bishops would die at the hands of Roman officials. Their tombs became liturgical shrines. The text of the liturgy began to include a list of early martyrs, heroes and heroines of the faith now invoked as part of the holy sacrifice of the Mass: "Peter and Paul, Andrew, James . . . Thomas, James, Philip, Bartholomew, Matthew, Simon and Jude . . . Linus, Cletus, Clement, Sixtus, Cornelius, Cyprian, Lawrence, Chrysogonus, John and Paul, Cosmas and Damian . . . John, Stephen, Matthias, Barnabas, Ignatius, Alexander, Marcellinus and Peter, Felicity and Perpetua, Agatha, Lucy, Agnes, Cecilia and Anastasia."

Roman authorities developed formalized tests to which they'd subject suspected Christians. One of the most common was demanding that Christians burn incense in worship before the emperor's statue. The reforming emperor Diocletian (284–305), who came to power after a century of almost constant civil war, was determined to elevate imperial authority to the heights once enjoyed by pharaohs in Egypt, whose subjects adored them as god-kings. His program could not abide an expanding class of citizens who rejected imperial godhead. Thus, the empire embarked on a massive, coordinated persecution of Christians, killing uncounted thousands. (Historians still argue over the actual numbers involved).[180]

Romans with little to live for and nothing to die for watched entranced as Christians stood courageously in the Colosseum, dying at the hands of wild beasts and gladiators. By this means, the blood of the martyrs would become the seed of the Church.

Religious Freedom at Last

The savagery aimed at Christians ended only with the rise to power of Constantine (306–337). As this soldier embarked on his own rebellion to claim the imperial throne, he experienced some epiphany. He would later recount a vision that promised him victory if he venerated the chi-rho, a common Christian symbol using Christ's initials. Victorious in the civil war that followed, he issued the historic Edict of Milan, granting Christians total religious freedom.

During his reign, Constantine went much further, leaning on the newly emancipated Christians as a key base of support.

Bishops went from the catacombs to the imperial palace and served Constantine as advisors. He paid to rebuild churches that the Roman state had destroyed.[181] He abolished the pagan sacrifices and rites long required for service in the army. Constantine summoned the Council of Nicaea, over which he presided (though still unbaptized) in an effort to resolve the savage divisions among believers over the divinity of Christ. That council codified our Creed and helped set the final canon of the New Testament, enshrining as inspired books the gospels and letters that had been used in major churches over previous centuries. Constantine's conversion set the tone for Rome's ruling class and his family, most of whom would join the newly legalized Church.

Constantine's conversion also laid the groundwork for a more ambiguous further development—the later emperor Theodosius's declaration that Christianity was the official religion of the empire. Theodosius (379–395) did more than favor Christians. He also persecuted pagans, closed down their temples, and imposed legal disabilities on Jews. Those actions reflected more the autocratic impulses of the empire than the spirit of the Gospel. But they set the stage for dangerous entanglements between Church and state.

All but one of the Roman emperors after Constantine were professed Christians. Christianity began to be enfolded into the fabric of the Roman state. Emperors abandoned the old laissez-faire approach to the religious beliefs of citizens. Instead, they saw religion as one more tool for encouraging social cohesion— or even ensuring that divine favor would aid the empire.

When the Arian heresy became widespread, a succession of Roman emperors embraced that doctrine. Suddenly Christians who affirmed the full divinity of Christ endured imperial persecution, as their ancestors had before Constantine. Conversely, orthodox emperors wielded the power of the state against heretics.

A Church that had asked only for liberty from pagan Roman emperors now urged their Christian successors to silence theological opponents. There is nothing in the New Testament on which Christians can ground such a policy. Jesus's preaching laid heavy emphasis on people's free decision to follow Him or turn away. Consider, for example, this passage in Luke:

When the days drew near for him to be received up, he set his face to go to Jerusalem. And he sent messengers ahead of him, who went and entered a village of the Samaritans, to make ready for him; but the people would not receive him, because his face was set toward Jerusalem. And when his disciples James and John saw it, they said, "Lord, do you want us to bid fire come down from heaven and consume them?" But he turned and rebuked them. And they went on to another village. (Luke 9: 51–56)

The first bishops to think of employing religious persecution got slapped down by Christ himself.

CHAPTER 10

FROM *THE CITY OF GOD* TO THE CRUSADES

B y the early fifth century, the Church had become impossibly entangled with the Roman Empire. The brilliant and vastly influential Christian theologian St. Augustine tried to extricate the Church in his epic work *The City of God.* In part, he wrote it to answer stubborn Roman pagan elites, who claimed that the growing chaos in the empire was the punishment for abandoning its ancestral gods (in whom almost no one still believed). The collapse was happening in the most pagan parts of the Empire, and Rome's military strength was greatest in the Christian East. Yet Augustine felt it necessary to respond to this slander nonetheless.

Regardless, the North African bishop countered by developing a sophisticated theory of overlapping citizenship. By virtue of their birth into a fallen world, all men are first citizens of the City of Man, which concerns itself solely with our temporal fortunes. Those baptized into Christ receive a new and higher citizenship in the City of God, whose concerns and fate are eternal. There was no guarantee, Augustine argued, that the interests of those two cities would coincide, nor that even a Christian empire would thrive against its enemies.

Unfortunately, Augustine contributed another, negative element to the picture. Frustrated by the dogged, sometimes violent Donatist heretics—rigorists who insisted that sacraments offered by sinful clergy were totally invalid—Augustine called on the Roman state to prosecute them. Here was the first statement by any eminent Christian leader justifying government regulation, and suppression, of Christians' religious practice. Arian and orthodox emperors had been using imperial force against dissenters long before Augustine called for suppressing the Donatist heretics. His arguments, however, would echo over the centuries and justify countless future uses of state power to settle religious disagreements.

Great Christian thinkers would feel bound by deference to Augustine and loyalty to a Church that regarded the forcible defense of orthodoxy as a duty of Christian rulers. Thomas Aquinas, Martin Luther, John Calvin, and the Anglican bishops of England would all affirm the role of the state in promoting religious uniformity. Since the age of the Byzantine emperor Theodosius, Christian rulers had seen preserving orthodoxy as part of their secular mission. Those who neglected repression of heretics were suspected of heresy themselves, or of a religious indifference that a just God would punish. So Christian kings in nations such as France would, in their coronation oaths, swear to extirpate heresy.

The problem? Granting the government competency to judge what would lead to salvation, and coercively enforce it, grossly trespassed on the freedom to believe on which Jesus seemed to insist. Indeed, we see here one of the origins of modern, secular totalitarianism.

The first Christians were executed for heresy some centuries after Augustine. The wielding of state power at the expense of Christian conscience—correct or mistaken—would become one of the greatest scandals in the history of the Church, leaving blood on the hands of Catholic, Protestant, and Orthodox rulers and churchmen alike. Each church would have its own martyrs at the hands of other churches, with mutual recriminations and bitter divisions resulting.

Only the mutual exhaustion of the Reformation and Counter-Reformation would lead Christians again to call for the state to restrict itself to protecting religious liberty.

Making Faith a Prop of the State

After the fall of Rome, the Christian Church that had converted the whole Roman Empire developed quite differently in each of the empire's two halves. In the eastern (or Byzantine) empire, where imperial authority managed to survive for another thousand years, the Church had to operate within the framework of a powerful, bureaucratic state. But the collapse of Rome left the Church in the West freer from secular interference. In fact, popes like Gregory the Great (590–604) had to restore a semblance of order in Rome, keeping the aqueducts flowing with water, the roads repaired, and some measure of law and order.

The first successful effort to build an extensive secular state in the West was the kingdom of the Franks. It covered what today is France, Germany, the Low Countries, Switzerland, Austria, and northern Italy. The Frankish monarchs forged a partnership with the papacy, replacing the distant Byzantines as protectors of Rome against invasion. The close cooperation between Frankish kings and popes culminated on Christmas Day in 800 with Pope Leo III crowning the Frankish monarch Charles (later Charlemagne) as "emperor." In other words, the heir to the long-vacant authority of Constantine, the highest Christian monarch in the West.

Though not a man of peace or a perfect husband, Charlemagne had a fervent religious commitment and focused on restoring culture. He tasked the Christian clergy with opening a network of schools, reorganizing Christian worship, and evangelizing pagans. He granted lands and wealth to clergy to make this possible, and the result was what scholars have called the "Carolingian Renaissance."

Charlemagne's empire shattered pretty quickly. But the pattern of the clergy working alongside kings and higher nobles to govern and educate the populace was set.[182]

Despite the influence the Holy Roman Empire exerted over the papacy, the political independence of the pope in faraway Rome guaranteed that the Church could never become a mere department of government. Indeed, bishops throughout the West often wielded the same independence and authority as feudal lords, sometimes commanding armies.

Clergymen's involvement in worldly affairs carried its dangers, of course. Yes, a bishop who became the feudal lord might rule a region more justly than an ordinary baron. On the other hand, he might begin to act and live like nothing more than a baron. Forbidden by canon law from carrying swords, warrior bishops would wield a mace, smashing heads in battle with all the gusto of any warlord. Many priests abandoned the apostolic practice of celibacy and began to marry, often deeding "their" parish to their first-born sons, as if the Christian priesthood were a Brahmin-style hereditary caste.

Meanwhile, the eastern half of the Roman Empire, based in Constantinople, would retain its integrity until 1453. The Byzantine Empire hosted and protected millions of Christians, and it created a rich, sophisticated culture that carried on the best traditions of antiquity. Unlike large swaths of the West, the East never saw the virtual collapse of literacy or the crumbling of central authority into feudalism.

Unfortunately, the very vigor of the Byzantine Empire meant that the Church in the East was much more subject to secular control. Emperors appointed and deposed bishops and even patriarchs, invented and enforced heresies, and persecuted religious dissenters across the empire's vast territories.

This would have unanticipated consequences. Groups that dissented from the official Church consensus on crucial doctrines didn't dry up and disappear. Instead, they operated underground and sometimes even colluded with foreign enemies of a Byzantine government they saw as a wicked persecutor.[183] The policy of repression, combined with high taxes and resentment at foreign rule, worked to weaken the eastern empire's hold over much of its southern territory. Orthodox bishops controlled most churches, with support from Byzantine armies, but much of the empire was a religious powder keg.

Islam's Global War on Every Other Religion

Then came the Muslims. In the seventh century, Arabs united around the newly invented creed of Muhammad. They rose up to overwhelm armies of both Byzantium and the Persian (Zoroastrian) empire, which had been engaged in a punishing, decades-long war.

Local Christians whose heretical creeds had made the local bishops and rulers their enemies sometimes greeted the Muslim troops as liberators. It would be far too late for second thoughts when these Muslim conquerors made clear their intentions: Non-Muslim monotheists (Christians and Jews) would be reduced to third-class citizenship, to a degraded condition we might compare to the treatment of blacks in Jim Crow America, known as "dhimmitude."[184]

Dhimmis had to pay a special tax to which Muslims were immune. They could not carry weapons or work in a long list of professions. They couldn't ride horses—only donkeys. They had to wear special clothing or badges and step aside to make way when any Muslim tried to pass. Their testimony in court did not have the same weight as Muslims', making them prey for legal mistreatment. They could not build new houses of worship or repair damage to old ones. They could not ring bells, hold religious processions, or obey the Great Commission of Jesus: preach the Gospel.

Most Muslim schools of sharia still maintain today that this is the proper relationship between Muslims and Christians, and the goal of Islamist activists is to see it imposed worldwide.

Christians, buttressed by the examples of the early Church's martyrs and by Jesus's own example, often resisted sudden, brutal persecution. But dhimmitude proved different. Over the centuries, most believers in the old heartlands of the Church—Iraq, Syria, Egypt, Palestine, and North Africa—drifted into Islam. The prospect of a quick, gory martyrdom is apparently less daunting than the grim knowledge that you, and your children, and your great-great grandchildren, will be subject to constant humiliation, subjugation, and shunning. Christians in today's West, subject to a secular sharia that targets faithful believers, should take warning from such history.

Islam teaches that every non-Muslim is a willful rebel against Allah. Both Judaism and Christianity, Muhammad taught, were latter-day corruptions of the original true religion: Islam. The highest vocation for any Muslim man was (and is to this day) fighting unbelievers in sacred Jihad, until the entire world embraces Islam or is willingly subjugated to Muslim rulers.

Jesus led no armies and forbade His apostles even to defend Him from false arrest. Muhammad had no such scruples, himself assembling armies and leading them into wars of conquest. Muhammad also ordered massacres of non-Muslims his armies had conquered, ethnically cleansing Arabia of both Christians and Jews.

The shocking, explosive attacks of suddenly united Arab tribes destroyed the Persian Empire and cut the size of the Byzantine Empire by two-thirds. Muslim regimes now ruled over the sullen populations of long-Christian cities, including most of those St. Paul named in his epistles. Two of the seats of Christian patriarchs, Jerusalem and Antioch, were firmly in Muslim hands. A third, Constantinople, was under siege—quite literally on two occasions, when the city almost fell to Arab invaders and their barbarian allies.

The degree of religious tolerance for Christians and Jews depended on the whims of individual monarchs. Some were more pious and exerted greater pressure to squeeze their subjugated non-Muslims to convert. Other rulers liked the extra taxes non-Muslims paid, so they preferred not to convert the geese that kept laying golden eggs.

A Papal Revolutionary

Complicating life for Christians further, Byzantine emperors interpreted Islam's conquests as God's judgment on the eastern empire's Christians for their attachment to religious imagery—to statues, icons, stained glass, and other representations of the sacred. The Muslims, who scorned all imagery, were winning wars, after all. Hence, emperors starting with Leo III (d. 741) banished from churches the icons beloved of ordinary Christians, destroying or whitewashing ancient images of Jesus and the saints.

In response to this imperial move, monks led mobs of believers against their iconoclastic bishops. Iconoclastic emperors found themselves denounced from popular pulpits. Eventually Byzantine elites saw that iconoclastic policies couldn't endure.

But they took from this whole crisis a lesson: control of the Church was essential to the smooth functioning of the state. The ruler of the secular state took on a quasi-priestly role. The emperor was the mediator of justice between heaven and earth, a figure of solemn religious importance. He summoned church councils. He appointed and could remove local bishops and even Patriarchs of Constantinople. The emperor's role was sacred as well as profane.

The already close relationship between Church and state in the East became even closer—and Church leaders increasingly became creatures of the state. (Even today, Russian and Ukrainian Orthodox bishops offer slavish support for their government's policies.)

A similar problem emerged in the West. Insofar as clergy filled vital roles in governance and wielded power, kings and lesser nobles sought to control them. The emperors in Germany, for instance, demanded and got the power to pick their local bishops—exactly as the emperors did in faraway Constantinople. By the tenth century, the papacy itself had fallen under the control of local warlords and aristocrats, who picked the popes—choosing pliant, corrupt puppets to serve as the earthly head of the Church. The only way to rescue the papacy from these small-time hoodlums? The German emperor invaded Italy, deposed several venal popes, and appointed better ones.

Now, a similar pattern had emerged in the Muslim caliphate, the highest religious authority for Sunni Muslims worldwide. Early on, this exalted office had fallen under the control of the most powerful Arab dynasty. Had the West followed this pattern, the spiritual authority of the Church would have become completely intertwined with the authority of the state. The ruling class's embrace of Christianity would have become ever more suffocating, as religious practice and even doctrine found itself twisted to serve the king's perception of the common good—or merely his power.

One man led a movement that halted this corruption. A learned and pious monk named Hildebrand fought worldliness and corruption among the clergy. He became so beloved in Rome that when the reigning pope died, the common people acclaimed Hildebrand as his successor. He took the name Pope Gregory VII in 1073.

Gregory decided that the Church had become entirely too comfortable, too this-worldly, too engaged in social work and power politics, to accomplish its sacred mission. He led a movement of fellow reform-minded clergy dedicated to marking off very clearly the spheres proper to Church and to state.[185]

Most important for subsequent history, Gregory announced that the spiritual power of the Church was separate from and higher than the authority of kings. While kings might claim to derive their power from God, popes and bishops received their missions and offices from Christ. Secular kings could no longer be allowed to control which bishops served in their lands, much less to depose and appoint popes.

This decree put Gregory on a collision course with the most powerful monarch in the West—Henry IV, the Holy Roman Emperor. To Henry, it was absurd that his government granted all manner of power and privileges to bishops but might lack the power to choose them.

Still, Gregory insisted on his decree liberating the Church from secular control. Henry responded by summoning his bishops and ordering them to declare Gregory deposed. A monarch with an army faced a lonely Roman cleric who had only his moral authority.

But such was the prestige and respect Gregory had earned that he prevailed. He excommunicated Henry and deposed him from the throne. This freed Henry's subjects from their loyalty oaths to the emperor and unwound his hold on his realm. Thus, it came about in 1077 that Emperor Henry had to travel the Alps in winter to the pope's residence in Canossa. The Emperor of the West knelt for three days in the snow before the pope emerged to absolve him. Yes, Henry would strike back later at the pope, and the conflict between the Church and the

Empire would continue. But it was clear from this moment on that in the West, the Church and her moral authority would compete against the power of warlords, kings, even emperors.

The Crusades: A War for Religious Freedom

In the eleventh century, four hundred years after the Muslim conquest, less-civilized Seljuk Turks from central Asia displaced the Arabs as rulers of the Holy Land in Palestine. These new Muslim conquerors massacred Christian pilgrims and renewed assaults on the remaining provinces of the Byzantine Empire. So in 1095, Byzantine emperor Alexios I, overlooking the religious schism that now divided his church from Rome's, wrote to Pope Urban II asking for aid. And the pope answered.

Most of the pagan kingdoms of western Europe had by now been Christianized. Consequently, when Pope Urban called on kings and nobles to free the Holy Places and aid the Christian Byzantines, many thousands of westerners answered.

In the era of highly decentralized feudal rule, constant fighting was the profession of men in the Christian noble classes. However steeped they might be in the rites and doctrines of Christian faith, knights and barons were also stained with the blood of their fellow Christians. These weren't just, defensive wars such as Augustine had specified Christians could fight. They were vicious squabbles over territory, fought for glory and profit.

We have countless tales of ruthless warlords conducting sieges that ended with mass slaughters, then seeking forgiveness for their sins. Before the Turkish conquest, penance for battlefield sins often took the form of pilgrimages to the Holy Land. In the best times, this was a life-endangering proposition, given the hazards of travel, exposure to strange diseases, and the real possibility that a baron might end up captured by Arabs and enslaved.[186]

Urban had the inspired idea (perhaps divinely inspired) to organize the feuding, guilt-ridden warriors of Christendom into a single holy pilgrimage. They would march to the aid of a Christian emperor and free the holy city of Jerusalem from its Muslim conquerors. They would aid the native Christians, ending their servitude, and establish free access for pilgrims to the sites of the life of Christ.

In short, the crusaders had genuinely religious motives, contrary to the centuries of distortion and outright slander that have accumulated around them.[187]

One common myth holds that the crusaders sought to plunder the Muslims to get rich. In fact, they typically bankrupted themselves to equip their entourages for the journey. Few expected to return home alive, so they left their estates with their heirs. When the First Crusade, through a series of seemingly miraculous events, succeeded in conquering both Antioch and Jerusalem, the crusaders set up feudal states—like those they knew back at home. But they did not persecute Muslims or even set out on a serious effort to convert them to Christianity. Instead, they established Christian states that broadly tolerated extensive religious differences.

There were appalling atrocities committed along the way— mostly by disorganized bands of commoners who attached themselves to the crusaders. Against the explicit orders of local bishops and Christian nobles, these mobs making their way pointlessly to the Holy Land sometimes attacked local Jews. Despite the best efforts of churchmen to protect these peaceful citizens, the mobs often prevailed. Contemporary Jewish chronicles of the Crusades understandably lay heavy emphasis on these atrocities, which Christian authorities condemned and tried to prevent.

Our picture of the Crusades today is jaundiced, viewed through many layers of hostile sentiment: anti-Catholicism, anti-Western multiculturalism, and secularist scorn for Christianity in particular. It's easy to focus on the slaughters that often ensued after lengthy sieges—and forget that these occurred just as often in Europe among fellow Christians, and invariably after Muslim sieges of Christian or Hindu cities. Such were the laws of war at the time, all around the world, much as we now deplore them.

But a broader and fairer view of the Crusades ought to see them at least as much as a long-delayed defensive counterattack on the part of Western man, and Christendom, after hundreds of years of almost uninterrupted Muslim aggression. The Christian volunteers willing to die in defense of their faith won religious freedom for Christians in the Middle East, at least for some time.

Are Tyrants Immune from Removal?

By the Middle Ages, no firm consensus had emerged among Christians in the West on the morality of rising up against unjust governments.

On one hand, monarchs had grown stronger. Kings' personal domains had multiplied, and they'd begun to have the cash to raise and maintain royal armies. They no longer needed to rely mostly on feudal levies of powerful magnates. Bishops also anointed kings, which granted secular rulers a certain sacerdotal protection that disgruntled subjects were (mostly) loath to violate.

On the other hand, periodic revolts by barons in various lands had reinforced firm limits on the powers of kings. The English Magna Carta (1215) resulted from the uprising of nobles disgusted by King John's financial rapacity and military incompetence. Tellingly, a cardinal and the Archbishop of Canterbury helped negotiate and draft the document.

Magna Carta outlined the rights properly due an Englishman by virtue of the country's (unwritten) constitution. It did not—and no document would, for several centuries—assert that such rights were proper to them as human beings, which anyone should enjoy regardless of his country. It would take the U.S. founding before a country affirmed such rights as part of its governing philosophy.

Magna Carta is justly revered as England's first institutional guarantee of subjects' rights, and of limits on royal privileges. The document forbade arbitrary imprisonment of Englishmen, guaranteed the rights of the Church, and offered protections for both free subjects and serfs. It granted to major barons the right to refuse new taxes—a right that in subsequent centuries would be extended to leading commoners in Parliament.

The document would take on more importance over time, as subsequent kings felt constrained to republish and reaffirm Magna Carta as the price of securing the throne. Kings who aspired to arbitrary rule would forbid discussion of it, while supporters of Parliament—and later, of independence for the American colonies—would cite the "Great Charter" as a long-revered legal precedent.

But limiting royal abuses was one thing. What about when a king ignored such constraints and behaved as an outright tyrant? A pope might declare a king excommunicate and his subjects absolved from their oaths. But he couldn't guarantee that those subjects would listen. And what if a king's abuses didn't focus on the Church, or if he'd made the pope an ally? Did subjects have any other recourse when a king violated basic rights?

The Duty to Resist a Wicked King

Medieval thinkers grappled with these questions. The first to advance the idea that citizens had the right or perhaps the duty to resist unjust commands by a superior, even a king, was the twelfth-century philosopher John of Salisbury. David Kopel offers a fascinating discussion of this thinker. Kopel writes of Salisbury's main work, *Policraticus* (published 1159):

John explained that a good Christian should not be expected to obey the law or a superior's order in all circumstances, for "Some things are . . . so detestable that no command will possibly justify them or render them permissible." For example, a military commander might order soldiers to deny the existence of God or to commit adultery. Similarly, if a prince "resists and opposes the divine commandments, and wishes to make me share in his war against God, then with unrestrained voice I must answer back that God must be preferred before any man on earth."

John argued that intermediate magistrates, such as local governors, had a duty to lead forcible resistance, if necessary, against serious abuses by the highest magistrate, such as the king.[188]

The doctrine that citizens can and must resist state-sponsored injustice goes back a lot longer than most modern people realize. This principle would find support in the greatest and most influential medieval thinker, St. Thomas Aquinas. Kopel cites the saint's reflection on whether subjects owed ongoing obedience to rulers who'd proven tyrannical. Although Aquinas treated "sedition," or arbitrary rebellion, as gravely sinful, he made room for legitimate resistance, even by force. In the *Summa Theologiae*, Aquinas wrote:

A tyrannical government is not just, because it is directed, not to the common good, but to the private good of the ruler. . . . Consequently, there is no sedition in disturbing a government of this kind, unless indeed the tyrant's rule be disturbed so inordinately, that his subject suffer greater harm from the consequent disturbance than from the tyrant's government.[189]

Here Aquinas is echoing Augustine—as he often does. The preconditions that Augustine set for a just war apply equally to a just civil war or revolution. A key criterion for either one is the prudent judgment of whether the war (of either kind) is proportionate to the evil it's meant to curb. Or is it merely a pretext? Worse, is the struggle clearly doomed, with no realistic prospect of success?

Jump ahead five hundred years, and you can hear an echo of these Natural Law precepts in the words of Thomas Jefferson's Declaration of Independence. Jefferson asserts that all men

are endowed by their Creator with certain unalienable Rights, that among these are Life, Liberty and the pursuit of Happiness. —That to secure these rights, Governments are instituted among Men, deriving their just powers from the consent of the governed, —That whenever any Form of Government becomes destructive of these ends, it is the Right of the People to alter or to abolish it, and to institute new Government, laying its foundation on such principles and organizing its powers in such form, as to them shall seem most likely to effect their Safety and Happiness.

But neither Jefferson nor Aquinas suggests that anarchy-minded citizens may undertake revolutions willy-nilly. Both thinkers set a high bar for embarking on such a grievous enterprise as civil war. Determining whether and when a political situation has become so "destructive" is a solemn and serious inquiry. Jefferson freely confesses this:

Prudence, indeed, will dictate that Governments long established should not be changed for light and transient causes; and accordingly all experience hath shewn, that mankind are more disposed to suffer, while evils are sufferable, than to right themselves by abolishing the forms to which they are accustomed. But when a long train of abuses and usurpations, pursuing invariably the same Object evinces a design to reduce them under absolute Despotism, it is their right, it is their duty, to throw off such Government, and to provide new Guards for their future security.

Indeed, it is Jefferson's task in the rest of the Declaration to establish the necessity, justice, and prudence of the united colonies' decision to cut all political ties to Britain. Most of the text is aimed at proving exactly this.

CHAPTER 11

RELIGIOUS LIBERTY, THE RIGHT TO RESIST TYRANNY, AND THE RIGHT TO BEAR ARMS

We can draw a line from Aquinas's reflections on resisting tyranny to the Declaration of Independence. Still, many other developments had to occur to produce an American political order that protected our God-given rights. The seismic events of the Reformation and the Counter-Reformation played an important role—in part because they unintentionally eroded the independence of churches.

Much like Pope Gregory VII in the late eleventh century, Martin Luther in the early sixteenth century saw a Church beset by worldliness and corruption. But whereas Gregory believed the Church had become too entangled with the state, Luther and others became disillusioned by the papacy itself.

The unintentional consequences of the Reformation arose because both Luther and his opponents turned to the power of the state to support their religious views.

Catholic bishops in Germany leaned on the Holy Roman Emperor, Charles V, to prosecute Luther for heresy. German nobles who resented papal taxes and approved of Luther's views offered him protection. Charles himself was eager to find some split-the-difference theological compromise to keep peace in his ramshackle empire.

After Luther was condemned at the Diet (congress) of Worms in 1521, Protestant nobles spirited him away to safety. Dukes, barons, and other local leaders encouraged Luther-inspired reforms, which just happened (by sheer coincidence) to strip bishops and monasteries of vast, valuable estates. (Pious folk wishing for prayers after their death had been leaving lands to the church for centuries, till religious institutions owned some one-third of the land in Europe.) On several occasions, promising compromises that might have healed the breach in the Church smashed on the rocks of property disputes: Catholic bishops demanded that the secular lords return the lands they'd seized, and they refused.

In Scandinavia and the estates of the Teutonic Knights, secular rulers saw Luther's ideas as the pretexts for massive land grabs and bringing the once-independent Church under royal control. The same thing happened in England under King Henry VIII, after his failed annulment case drove that once-convinced Catholic to reject papal authority.

In countries where the monarchs remained in communion with Rome, the Church lost its previous freedom of action and independent influence. The pope found that his threats of excommunication frightened no one, and he had to tread lightly with monarchs in France and Spain, lest they decide to pull a Henry VIII themselves. So Catholic monarchs gained control over who got appointed bishop. In effect, the French or Spanish king had the same power over the local church as Henry had seized in England. The kings could even veto or censor official Church documents. (The reforming Council of Trent would not see its documents published in Spain for many decades, since the Spanish king didn't approve of them.)

Luther's radical challenge to the practices and preaching of a thousand years proved to be a political catalyst, too. If the hierarchy of the Church could be challenged, why not that of the state? Of society and the economy? If the claims of the pope and bishop were not sanctified by God, what about the claims of feudal lords to take large portions of the crops their serfs grew? A massive social revolt began in fragmented, religiously divided Germany, with peasants expropriating their overlords by violent force.

Luther was horrified by what his revolt had unleashed. He sided with the barons, denouncing the social revolutionaries who'd cited his example and calling on local lords to crush the

Peasants' Revolt. He adopted a theology that was essentially quietist on politics. God had appointed the rulers of the secular realm to keep order, and rebellion against such leaders was sinful in itself.

Both Lutherans and Catholics strove to win over secular rulers, to wield the sword of the state to impose their religious programs on all their fellow citizens. No religious leader, Catholic or Protestant, advocated the kind of personal and corporate religious liberty we now take for granted. They saw religious orthodoxy as one of the social goods God meant for the government to ensure.

A century after Luther, the enormously complex and murderous Thirty Years' War (1618–1648) saw Catholic France join the Protestant powers in Europe to oppose the Habsburg monarchy. The Habsburgs controlled much of Germany as well as Spain and Portugal—and those two kingdoms' massive New World empires. Because the combatants believed they were fighting for eternal truths on which the salvation of millions depended, the war was fought with unparalleled ruthlessness. Entire cities burned, as conquering armies put "heretics" to the sword, be they civilian or soldier.

The resolution of that war satisfied no one, but it established a kind of peace. The prince of any polity, large or small, would determine the religion that prevailed there. Those who disagreed must submit or emigrate. Political power thus reigned supreme over a church that had lost almost all its institutional power and independence.

There were, however, two movements that dissented from the consensus. They suggested that citizens had the right to rebel against governments that suppressed their religious faith. And it's from these two movements that we can trace the first glimmers of religious liberty such as we know it today—a foundational element of the philosophy of freedom that animated America's Founders. In one of history's ironies, these movements were mortal enemies: the Calvinists and the Jesuits.

The Churches Compelled to Discover Religious Liberty

It would take hundreds of years of grueling conflict for various churches and nations to accept that religious liberty, both individual and corporate, was essential to civil peace. Only once brute reality had made such liberty necessary in practice would Christian thinkers finally admit that it was correct in principle, too—that it was the proper extension of the Christian view of the person. Crucially for our purposes in this book, those who called for religious liberty developed the arguments that ordinary citizens might rebel against the government to demand their religious freedom.

The strong religious arguments against the dominion of king over clergy came from members of disfavored, minority religions. These religious dissenters typically were not Lutherans, most of whom lived in territories controlled by friendly princes. In any case, Luther's theology after the Peasants' Revolt did not venture into justifications for social revolution. But Calvinists living under persecution in Catholic France, as well English Catholic Jesuits (in exile or underground), did precisely that. As David Kopel recounts, these were the thinkers to develop Thomas Aquinas's medieval argument that kings who descended into tyranny ought to lose their thrones or lives. Kopel traces the growth of this argument in great scholarly detail.[190]

For France's Calvinists—known as the Huguenots—violence and even war became a regular feature of life. Between 1562 and 1598, France collapsed into episodic religious civil conflict: the Wars of Religion. The Huguenots never won. Radical Catholic nobles and mobs sometimes subjected them to organized massacres. The worst of these was the infamous St. Bartholomew's Day Massacre (1572), in which the French crown colluded in the gangland-style killings of thousands of Calvinists across the country.

French Calvinists went into exile and started writing. In 1573, legal scholar François Hotman published *Francogallia*, which, in Kopel's words, "argued that France's ancient constitutional law recognized the separation of powers and the right of the people to overthrow a bad dynasty." John Calvin had already written that it was the duty of "lesser magistrates" (public officials) to protect the people's liberties from a wicked, tyrannical king. Calvin's successor as leader of the Reformed church, Theodore Beza, expanded on this theory. Citing the Book of Samuel, where the king was the choice of the people, "Beza said that the people and king were bound to each other by covenant," Kopel explains. Beza concluded that the people, acting through "intermediate magistrates," had "the right to remove the crown they had awarded if the king did not obey his part of the covenant."[191]

Advancing the argument still further was a Huguenot writer using the pen name Marcus Junius Brutus (Caesar's assassin). His 1579 book *Vindiciae Contra Tyrannos* agreed that the people's magistrates could overthrow a king for violating his covenant (and their freedom to practice the true religion). Crucially, as Kopel notes, Brutus went beyond biblical and historical arguments to ground this right of the people. Brutus wrote: "[N]atural law teaches us to preserve and protect our life and liberty—without which life is scarcely life at all—against all force and injustice. Nature implants this in dogs against wolves . . . the more so in man against himself, if he has become a wolf to himself."[192]

Brutus's book would be translated into English and widely popular in England, where the regime persecuted both Catholics and dissenting (Calvinist) Protestants.

The plight of English Catholics after Elizabeth I took the throne provoked similar reflections. The militant Society of Jesus provided most of the exiled missionaries willing to enter England and risk a slow death by disembowelment for "treason." (That, rather than heresy, was the crime for which Elizabeth executed Catholics.)

The Jesuits were an international order directly under the control of the pope, not local bishops. Their missions extended from Japan and China, to the new French settlements in North America, to Spanish conquests in South America. Thus, Jesuits were more prone than other clergy to question the actions of royal officials and the prerogatives of kings, especially where these interfered with the freedom of the Church. Indeed, this tendency toward internationalism and loyalty to the Church would lead Enlightenment monarchs to strong-arm the Vatican into suppressing the Jesuits by the late eighteenth century.

One of the most influential Jesuit theologians was Cardinal Robert Bellarmine. In his late-sixteenth-century work *De Summo Pontifice*, Bellarmine argued (in Kopel's words) "that subjects have no obligation to obey a ruler who is a heretic." Kopel continues: "At the pope's discretion, such a ruler could be deposed. Bellarmine urged Catholics to ignore King James I's requirement that they swear an oath of allegiance."[193]

Following in Bellarmine's tradition, Jesuits in Spain emphasized the people's authority over monarchs. Juan de Mariana made this case in *De Rege et Regis Institutione* (1599). Kopel summarizes Mariana's argument: "If a tyrant prevented intermediate bodies, such as the French Estates or the Spanish *cortes* [parliament], from assembling, a private individual would have the right to kill the tyrant." Kopel adds: "Mariana . . . was called the 'prophet of tyrannicide.' The Jesuits were accordingly considered subversive of existing governments."[194]

No doubt. In a bitter irony, the suppression of the Jesuits in France and other countries happened just two decades before the French Revolution. That's when a generation that had arisen without Jesuit education looked at the monarchy and the Church alike with angry, intolerant eyes. The revolution that ensued would yield a tyranny worse than anyone had ever known in Europe, the rule of alleged "Reason" that brooked no dissent whatsoever.

The English Civil War

Wars of Religion tore France apart in the sixteenth century. In the seventeenth century, it was England's turn.

The conflict in England was driven only partly by religious differences. There was much more at stake in the battles between Parliament and the Stuart monarchy, and the outcome was more complex. The messiness of the English Reformation and the complexities of England's constitutional history made sure of that. And we are all the forgetful beneficiaries.

As Kevin Phillips makes clear in his masterful popular history *The Cousins' Wars*, many non-doctrinal issues divided the supporters of the Stuart kings James I, Charles I, Charles II, and James II from the backers of parliamentary supremacy.[195] Social and economic factors played a role, too. Those who favored a powerful king with his own source of funds, not beholden to Parliament, tended to be rural, and they included members of the gentry and nobility, as well as peasants. The House of Commons, by contrast, was dominated by city-dwellers, merchants. These were "new men" who expected their wealth to grant them concomitant political power. This would often come at the expense of aristocrats and farmers.

Royalists did tend to be high-church Anglicans and persecuted Catholics, while parliamentarians were dominated by various shades of Calvinists, congregationalists, and separatist Protestants. Of course, such Protestants founded the first English colonies in New England.

As in France a hundred years before, nobody in the English conflict was fighting for religious liberty as we know it. Each side (including the Catholics living underground or in Ireland) was competing to place someone of its persuasion in power, then to use the state to pressure the rest of the population to conform. It was only the repeated failures of various factions to achieve this outcome that led to toleration, then protection, of religious minorities—as a "least-bad" outcome preferable to ongoing civil war. Our American religious settlement would be an outgrowth of what worked in England.

In most European countries, Catholic and Protestant, royal regimes in the seventeenth century gained power at the expense of aristocrats, the church, and medieval representative bodies such as parliaments. Autocratic monarchies were the "progressive" wave of the future, making possible the marshaling of national power and economic growth.

England was one of the great exceptions. In founding the Church of England, Henry VIII had undoubtedly strengthened the power of the throne. But he and his successors had also planted time bombs that would tick away over the decades. Queen Elizabeth I achieved what seemed a clever political compromise: retaining most church ritual and structure while making room for Calvinist theology. But the Church of England created to serve the royal regime was neither Catholic fish nor Protestant fowl. Instead, it was a battleground between those with quasi-Catholic understandings of theology and fiercely Calvinist reformers, both enrolled in the very same church, which claimed a national monopoly.

The compromise could not long endure.

Is the Executive Above the Law?

In the early 1600s, parliamentary supporters confronted a monarch, James I, who put forth a political theory he called "the Divine Right of Kings." On this view, the king embodied the law itself, which was identical to his will. Obedience to God required obedience to His appointed ruler on earth, leaving no justification for resistance or revolt.

As Kopel notes, James's theory was new to Englishmen, but it had ancient precedent. The absolute power of Roman emperors, oriental monarchs, and other pre-Christian rulers was still the norm outside of Europe, even in the seventeenth century. It was only the collapse of the Roman Empire that allowed for much more decentralized political institutions to emerge in the West. The rediscovery of Roman law during the Renaissance gave monarchs a powerful weapon in their quest to consolidate power.

As we saw, the shattering of the Church in the Reformation ended its political independence and made it subject to state control and interference. Throughout Continental Europe, except in the fractured Holy Roman Empire—which effectively ceased to function as a state—monarchs shook off medieval checks and balances on their power, and they imposed religious homogeneity through established, intolerant churches.

James I hoped to codify this sort of power through his Divine Right of Kings. Rallying to the king's cause were aristocrats, peasants, Catholics, and high-church Anglicans, who feared that the power of Parliament would benefit city dwellers, merchants (including slave traders), *nouveau riche* speculators, and radical Protestants.

But the idea of absolute power did not sit well with James's parliamentary opponents, many of them religiously motivated. With the Reformation continuing in England, variants of Christian belief and worship had emerged that were much more radical than the Anglican compromise that Queen Elizabeth had effected and that the king tried to enforce. James repressed these "Puritans," whose Calvinist theology and proto-democratic structure didn't fit the Anglican monarch's program. He repressed Catholics as well.

Calvinists and Catholics quickly denounced the Divine Right of Kings. They were determined to prevent the monarch from gaining so much power. The dispute continued into the reign of James's son and successor, Charles I.

What specific arguments did parliamentary supporters cite in defense of restricting royal power? Conservative scholar Russell Kirk has pointed out, in his indispensable history *America's British Culture*, a powerful irony that has had profound implications for all English-speaking countries: The most radical British Protestants looked to medieval precedents and institutions for legal arguments to frustrate the power of monarchs whom they viewed as both too powerful and too pro-Catholic. This meant that Protestant polemics drew on arguments of Catholic origins to make the case for the separation of powers.[196]

Radical Protestants cited Jesuit Robert Bellarmine and other Catholic thinkers on the God-given limits of royal power. Kopel writes:

> In 1644, the Scottish Presbyterian Samuel Rutherford published *Lex, Rex: or the Law and the Prince.* The point of the title was that the law precedes the king: the monarch must obey the law. In fact, the law is the ultimate king, above any human monarch. *Lex, Rex* refuted Charles I's bold assertion, articulated by an absolutist judge, that *rex est lex loquens*—that is, the king is the law speaking.
>
> The antecedent for *rex est lex* was the despotism of the late Roman Empire. The antecedent for *Lex, Rex* was the Old Testament. There, the very definition of the Hebrew nation is the people who live according to the law given by God. The Anglo-American ideal of the "rule of law" embodies Rutherford's principle. . . . [S]overeignty was inherent in the people, and was granted only conditionally to kings by the people.[197]

Arguments like Rutherford's were widely published and proved persuasive. Such arguments, in which radical Protestant rebels drew on medieval Catholic precedents, would have profound consequences in the long term. It would ultimately yield, in America, a situation of unprecedented freedom for churches and individual believers, which even the papacy would recognize. The United States was the first country in centuries where the Vatican could choose bishops freely, without government meddling. As Samuel Gregg recounts in *Tea Party Catholic*, the U.S. Congress in 1789 was puzzled when a letter arrived from the papal secretary, seeking permission to appoint the first Archbishop of Baltimore after the American Revolution. Congress wrote back, explaining that it had no power or wish to interfere.[198]

The arguments on limiting royal power proved consequential in the short term as well. Repeated efforts by Charles I to establish the monarchy as independent of Parliament, able to tax and raise armies without its consent, eventually led to civil war. After a bloody, back-and-forth struggle of several years, Parliament prevailed. Charles I was tried for treason and executed.

Fits and Starts

The English republic that emerged from this savage conflict might have honored representative principles. But its new polity represented only certain sectors of society. Its rule rested on fragile compromises among various sects of Protestants, some much more radical than others.

The differing views eventually paralyzed Parliament, and power fell into the hands of the capable Oliver Cromwell. He ruled for five years as a virtual military dictator, without consulting Parliament. Cromwell rode roughshod over Catholics, high-church Anglicans, and many other sectors of British society, who never recognized the legitimacy of his government. Some in the Anglican Church began to speak of "Charles I, King and Martyr."

Theocratic temptations emerged during Cromwell's regime, which banned theatrical shows and tried to suppress popular celebrations such as May Day and even Christmas as "papist" or pagan. Cromwell's efforts to suppress mostly Catholic, pro-royalist Ireland were particularly brutal, helping cement the bitterness against English rule that would eventually ensure Irish independence.

During Cromwell's reign, new, radical voices were heard. One of the most consequential was that of the genius poet John Milton, a genuine Renaissance man and fervent republican. He published a series of pamphlets in defense of his political ideas, the most influential of which was *Areopagitica*, which laid out the strongest case yet argued for an almost new idea: the freedom of the press, the publication of ideas from any citizen without prior approval from the government. Our own First Amendment owes its origin in part to this document.

Upon Cromwell's death in 1658, a groundswell of support arose for a return to normalcy, to the old English system of balance between a limited monarch and Parliament. The exiled Stuart heir to Charles I, his son Charles II, offered to restore that if given the throne. He returned in 1660, promising a moderate regime, which would rule with consent of Parliament, and amnesty for all the rebels—except those directly responsible for killing Charles I. That was a program most English were glad to accept.

But Charles II grew unhappy with the arrangement. He had spent his exile in France, where the monarchy had become absolute, with a dominion over the Church which not even the pope could challenge. King Louis XIV, who had hosted and supported Charles, didn't even summon France's parliament. His monarchy had vast estates and funds, and it ruled by decree. It resolved religious dissent by simple force, revoking the century-old toleration of French Protestants. The vicious persecution of Huguenots shocked the pope, who loudly condemned it. But France's king answered to no one, and thousands of French Protestants were stripped of their children (whom others would raise as Catholics), executed, or driven out of France.

Charles saw that his native Anglican Church was by no means as powerful or pliable as the Catholic Church in France. He married a French Catholic bride and secretly promised (in return for a stipend from France) to restore Britain to Catholicism whenever he possibly could. What is more, he lacked legitimate children, and his openly Catholic brother, James the Duke of York, was his only heir.

The reign of Charles II saw a cash-strapped king trying to patch back together the resources to make his throne independent of Parliament—exactly as his father, Charles I, had tried to do. He repressed the low-church or separatist Protestant churches that had supported Oliver Cromwell. He built up a private standing army, with many Irish Catholics in its ranks, to support the royal cause in case of rebellion.

The Price of the English Throne Was Guaranteeing Gun Rights

Parliament's ultimate victory over the Divine Right of Kings was driven largely by concerns of low-church, "dissenting" Protestants that the Anglican Church would continue or escalate its repression. Or even that the Catholic-friendly Stuarts might restore links with Rome and impose Catholicism on Britain.

When Charles II died (converting to Catholicism on his deathbed), his throne went to his Catholic brother, James II. James promised religious freedom for all and even tried to enlist as allies "dissenting" Protestants—offering them the same exemption from Anglican repression that he intended to offer Catholics.

But suspicion of the crown ran far too deep. James was, as his brother had been, closely allied with Louis XIV, even depending on him for financial subsidies. The French king's hands were stained deep red with Huguenot blood, and British Protestants were terrified that James intended to use French methods to restore Britain to Rome. When his wife bore a son and ensured a Catholic succession, Protestant nobles and leaders of Parliament approached James's Protestant daughter

Mary and her husband, William of Orange, who ruled in the Netherlands.

In 1688, the couple led the largest invasion fleet in British history from Holland across the English Channel. Most of James's army deserted him, and he fled to Catholic Ireland. There he lost a brief civil war with William and sailed off into exile.

What might surprise readers today is this: Pope Innocent XI had openly backed William's invasion, perhaps even secretly funding it. He issued a papal medal celebrating the Protestant victory. Innocent saw James as the puppet of Louis XIV, whose clumsy persecution of the Huguenots had embarrassed the Church, and whose constant interference in the Church's self-governance Innocent viewed as a greater threat than a Protestant king for England.

The British Parliament offered William the throne—but not without imposing a long list of conditions that limited royal power: the English Bill of Rights. This document was the seventeenth-century answer to Magna Carta, which conditioned the throne on the guarantee of certain basic rights. Unlike that medieval charter, it extended those rights to the population generally. And it would serve as the model, a century later, for America's crucial founding documents.

As the Declaration of Independence would, the English Bill of Rights laid out the reasons why a monarch's subjects (in this case, James II's) accused him of tyranny. As the American Bill of Rights would do, the English document spelled out certain fundamental liberties that the new regime promised to respect, as the basis of its legal legitimacy. These liberties included the free election of members to Parliament, without royal interference; a ban on a standing army in time of peace; a guarantee of fair, jury trials and reasonable bail; a prohibition on royal fund-raising without Parliament; and many other tenets that Americans would find familiar.

But the key element for us today is this one: *"That the subjects which are Protestants may have arms for their defence suitable to their conditions and as allowed by law."*

As Americans accustomed to, even spoiled by, the expansive religious freedom our forefathers purchased for us, we might read this provision cynically. Why is it limited to Protestants? Was it right to deny the same liberties to Catholics or Jews? But that is to ignore the historical context—which is crucial. Britain was exiting a period of religiously motivated civil war, in which Catholic-friendly kings allied to foreign Catholic monarchs who persecuted Protestants had selectively disarmed low-church Protestants. Indeed, under Charles II, royal representatives honeycombed Britain, seizing stores of gunpowder, rifles, cannons, and pistols, from Puritans, Presbyterians, and other supporters of the radical Reformation whom Charles suspected might back rebellion. Being disarmed left these persecuted groups potentially vulnerable to massacres by Catholics (as had happened in Ireland). For Protestants to feel safe in their practice of their religion, they needed private firearms.

But the English Bill of Rights did not affirm the right to armed self-defense merely as a reaction to the abuses of a particular king. Rather, Protestant thinkers—again, drawing on medieval Catholic precedents—saw the right to resist unjust royal power as a logical extension of what David Kopel calls the "natural right of self-defense." In *Lex, Rex: or the Law and the Prince*, Samuel Rutherford wrote of the fundamental danger of disarming the people: "To denude the people of [arms] because they may abuse the prince, is to expose them to violence and oppression, unjustly: for one king may more easily abuse [arms] than all the people; one may more easily fail than a community."[199] The long, tragic historical record of tyrants disarming and then persecuting the people reveals the wisdom of Rutherford's claim.

In her exquisitely detailed account *To Keep and Bear Arms: The Origins of an Anglo-American Right*, historian and constitutional scholar Joyce Lee Malcolm shows that notions of a right to bear arms did not emerge from the ether. She goes back to the Middle Ages, tracing the legal duties of Englishmen to practice the longbow and revealing shifting legal opinions about private ownership of newly invented firearms. But Malcolm also demonstrates that the first definitive assertion of a basic right to possess private firearms dates to this moment in history when Britain's new monarchs agreed to the English Bill of Rights.[200]

The provision in the English Bill of Rights about arms for defense would serve as the direct inspiration of the Second Amendment to the U.S. Constitution, which would make no discriminatory exceptions. The very fact that the founders of Britain's limited monarchy in 1689 saw religious freedom as dependent on citizens' right to arms ought to tell us something.

Our Founders saw it. Without a Second Amendment, we wouldn't long have a First.

The Founders knew it because they were well versed in the particular lessons of English history. In fact, the English Protestants who settled the North American colonies had watched with great anxiety from across the Atlantic as the Stuarts tried to impose political absolutism and religious conformity. The colonies in New England, full of Puritans and other "separatists," made open common cause with the parliamentary faction that overthrew and beheaded King Charles I. On the Restoration, several of the judges who'd passed sentence on Charles fled to friendly colonies such as Connecticut and Virginia. The overthrow of James II as king in Britain had been foreshadowed by violent resistance to his arbitrary rule in New England.[201]

CHAPTER 12

FROM THE MAYFLOWER COMPACT TO THE SECOND AMENDMENT

O
n November 11, 1620, on a ship at sea, America's answer to Magna Carta was born. It appeared in the form of a short document—a covenant, really, between the Pilgrims who'd fled persecution in England and the "strangers" (artisans and other essential workmen) who'd joined them for the journey. After storms blew the ship off course—for wintry New England instead of balmy Virginia—the men had been at each other's throats.[202]

This document was meant as a kind of peace treaty, to keep the company alive till they finally sighted land. More than that, it would serve as the moral basis for social and political order thereafter. Likewise, the mission of that community of Pilgrims would serve as the template for the entire American founding. The New England colonies would pioneer the fight against Parliament's power on American shores.

I speak of the Mayflower Compact. Once a staple of America's history classrooms, this document has almost been forgotten, despite how central the Pilgrims were to America's dawning identity.

Yes, many other communities would be founded, for many diverse reasons—from Catholic-friendly Maryland to the refuge for indentured servants that became the slave state of Georgia. As David Hackett Fisher explains in fascinating detail in *Albion's Seed*,[203] there were four broad groups of settlers whose original folkways and worldviews flowed like creeks to form the mainstream of early American culture:

- The Puritans of Massachusetts, who'd largely traveled from East Anglia, England. These religious separatists were the "Reformation of the Reformation." Back home, their faction was fighting against the power of England's king to control local churches' faith and worship. They would within twenty years wage and win a civil war that ended with the beheading of King Charles I.
- The Cavaliers of the upper South, and their indentured servants, who'd come from the south of England. These people hailed from regions and classes that would support the royal and Anglican

cause in the English Civil War. But they were keen to acquire property and protect their property rights. The experience of local self-government in colonies like Virginia would form them as ready opponents to British efforts to micromanage and tax the colonists from London.

- The Quakers of Pennsylvania, who sought and found religious freedom in America. This group's quietism and pacifism would keep them from playing a major role in the War of Independence. Their importance would emerge later on, in the founding of business and educational ventures and the dawning abolitionist movement.

- The Scots-Irish, who would settle the frontier areas of the South. These clannish, fiercely independent and individualistic settlers would form the backbone of Southern culture, apart from the genteel Tidewater aristocrats. Country music, "redneck" stereotypes, charismatic churches, and other features of what today's elitists consider "deplorable" can be traced to this settler subculture.

The Mayflower Compact was the first document of popular government in American history. Unlike the royal charters of various colonies, the compact emerged from the ground up instead of from the top down. Let's read its terms, with an eye to how the themes laid out here would play out in subsequent centuries:

In the Name of God, Amen. We whose names are underwritten, the loyal subjects of our dread Sovereign Lord King James, by the Grace of God of Great Britain, France, and Ireland King, Defender of the Faith, etc.

Having undertaken, for the Glory of God and advancement of the Christian Faith and Honour of our King and Country, a Voyage to plant the First Colony in the Northern Parts of Virginia, do by these presents solemnly and mutually in the presence of God and one of another, Covenant and Combine ourselves together into a Civil Body Politic, for our better ordering and preservation and furtherance of the ends aforesaid; and by virtue hereof to enact, constitute and frame such just and equal Laws, Ordinances, Acts, Constitutions and Offices, from time to time, as shall be thought most meet and convenient for the general good of the Colony, unto which we promise all due submission and obedience.

In witness whereof we have hereunder subscribed our names at Cape Cod, the 11th of November, in the year of the reign of our Sovereign Lord King James, of England, France and Ireland the eighteenth, and of Scotland the fifty-fourth. Anno Domini 1620.

Yes, the signers doffed their caps to the king. But he did not serve as the source of public order. The signers agreed to "Combine ourselves together into a Civil Body Politic." They, and not the English Parliament, would "enact, constitute and frame such just and equal Laws." This was a social contract.

These Pilgrims went on to found a political community in the wilds of Massachusetts *ex nihilo*, and to mold it according to experiment and experience. Their example would influence many other colonies. Crucially, pioneers who'd go on to settle the great American Middle West would largely come from New England—fleeing its stony, unyielding soil for vast, fertile prairies. They'd bring to the new American states much of the Puritan heritage of self-government and Christian mission.

The American Exception

What's really distinctive about America, even setting it apart from other English-speaking democracies, emerged from the events of the seventeenth century. Namely, the ongoing struggle between royal power and Parliament's, between the "high" Anglican church and "low" church Protestants, between rural gentry and capitalists based in cities.

And at crucial moments in that ongoing struggle, the question of the right to self-defense would be intertwined with religious freedom. Communities threatened with persecution would try to defend themselves against either royal power or hostile, intolerant mobs. Those without access to weapons would fail.

The Second Great Awakening would see the faith of the Puritans in New England spread all through the colonies, seeding the middle colonies and the South with independent, entrepreneurial churches. The religious preoccupations and fierce independence of the New England Protestants would thus inflect much of America.

In a sense, we are all the heirs of the Pilgrims on the *Mayflower*. And the Second Amendment that uniquely protects our right to keep and bear arms is the fruit of the sober, watchful concern for religious freedom that obsessed our Founding Fathers.

After the coup that installed William and Mary, American colonies could point to the very legal basis for the new British monarchy as a guarantee of their rights. The legitimacy of the new dynasty rested on its adherence to the English Bill of Rights—not to the hereditary rights of the Stuarts, who were in exile. The ideas and arguments of the parliamentary faction, later called the Whigs, pervaded the colonies. The new settlements had few high-churchmen, Tories, or defenders of royal absolutism.

In the influential New England colonies, the founding of towns usually went hand in hand with the planting of churches. For more than a hundred years, citizens' militias were almost entirely responsible for defending those colonies against Indian attacks and incursions by French or other European settlers.

Churches played a key role in organizing such militias, not just in Massachusetts but also in the predominantly Anglican Virginia. A regular theme of preaching in Protestant churches up and down the eastern seaboard was the moral and Christian duty of citizens to take part in the militias. Political scientist Ellis Sandoz's collection *Political Sermons of the American Founding Era* includes many such pastoral adjurations. The preachers explained that physically able men were obliged not just by their neighbors but by God to defend their settlements against outside attack—and implicitly against any attempts by a hostile government to restrict their religious freedom, local autonomy, and rights as British subjects as guaranteed in 1689.[204]

American settlers saw their political and religious liberties as seamlessly linked to each other, and churches as natural sites for them to gather in their defense.

The Social Contract Is Really a Covenant

While settlers in America embraced their right to keep and bear arms, a thinker on the other side of the Atlantic was further developing the case for citizens' rights in the face of absolute governments. The English political philosopher John Locke (1632–1704) would become a crucial source of arguments for opponents of absolute monarchy and religious coercion—not least the American Founders.

In recent years, a controversy has emerged around Locke's thought and his influence on America's founding. Channeling a reading of Locke's work by the brilliant but often perverse political theorist Leo Strauss, Catholic integralists have denounced Locke. For instance, Patrick Deneen, author of

Why Liberalism Failed, has claimed in many venues that Locke's worldview is only cosmetically different from the nihilistic atomism of Thomas Hobbes.[205] Deneen argues that Locke's apparently devout Protestant faith did not deeply infuse his writing on politics or prevent him from crafting a political system that would lead inevitably to same-sex marriage, abortion, and transgenderism.

Full-on Catholic integralists believe that the ideal political system would rest on divine Revelation (as interpreted by the popes) as well as the Natural Law that conservatives have traditionally seen as the basis of positive (that is, written, enforceable) law. Because they endorse the political enforcement of beliefs dependent on divine Grace, rather than reason, it is fair to call them proponents of Catholic sharia.

Their claims about Locke don't hold up either. Scholar Robert Reilly decisively dissects the arguments of Deneen and his allies in *America on Trial*.[206] Reilly shows that a) Locke was far from the main source of American liberty arguments, which drew from many authorities, and b) Locke depended on the biblical view of man, and biblical morality, to ground his arguments for human dignity and natural rights such as life, liberty, and property.

Similarly, in the book *God, Locke, and Liberty*, Joseph Loconte echoes the claim I've elaborated in this book: namely, that the classical liberal project of delineating and defending the rights of the individual depends entirely on the Christian view of the human person.[207] Materialism (be it Classical or Darwinist) does not yield inalienable human rights. Where on earth would they come from? There should be no surprise then that materialist regimes of the twentieth century behaved tyrannically. They did not see the vast dignity with which God crowned His creation, man. Although the Fall gravely injured our nature, it did not turn us into termites, ants, or other social insects better suited to domination and blind obedience. Furthermore, the Redemption that came with Christ restored our original dignity and in fact elevated it, by reason of Jesus now sharing a human nature with us.

Loconte shows in learned detail how Locke was formed by the Christian Humanist tradition of the Renaissance, especially the writings of the Catholic reformer Erasmus. That tradition emphasized in the political sphere the crucial role served by the free exchange of ideas and rational argument, rather than top-down coercion, censorship, official indoctrination, or persecution of "error." This tradition went somewhat underground after the religious wars and mutual persecutions of the Reformation and Counter-Reformation. But it reemerged strongly in England around the time of its civil wars.

Just as important was the religious dimension of the Renaissance tradition. As Loconte shows, the Renaissance Christian Humanists emphasized the ethical dimensions of the Gospel first, without rejecting the doctrinal truths asserted by Christian orthodoxy. Men like Erasmus and Thomas More urged a certain modesty about the human power to attain certitude about every particular concerning the profound mysteries of the divine nature. Instead of enlisting secular kings to persecute fellow Christians who might disagree about abstruse doctrinal issues, the Humanists urged Christians to pursue unity and cooperation on the broad swaths of moral truth where agreement ought to be easy.

John Locke took up their mantle and laid out the theoretical basis for the compromise that would come to dominate the English-speaking world: a broad tolerance of Protestant believers (and later of Catholics) and a newly tolerant attitude toward Jews and other non-Christians. Locke grounded his case not in mere practicality—exhaustion after centuries of persecution and counter-persecution —but in philosophy. In his *Letter Concerning Toleration* (1689), he argued that the real nature of Christian faith demanded freedom and that state interference in religious belief and preaching threatened the integrity of Christianity itself. It also violated the God-given rights of men, Locke said.[208]

From Loconte's work, we can see that the social contract Locke proposed as the basis of political legitimacy was not a secular construct like Thomas Hobbes's system. Instead, it was an echo of previous covenant theories of government that Christian writers (Catholic and Protestant) had grounded in the precedents of the Old Testament.

Now, in the *Letter Concerning Toleration*, Locke exempted Catholics from the broad religious freedom he proposed that Englishmen should enjoy. This is a flaw in his work, but not an incomprehensible one. Locke had witnessed France's fierce persecution of native Protestants, so he doubted the capacity of Catholic regimes to practice tolerance. As it happened, it would take almost three hundred years for the Catholic Church to officially embrace religious liberty in principle, at Vatican II.

The new model of religious tolerance would likewise unfold gradually. Restrictions on various churches fell away in some places more slowly than in others. Catholic services would remain illegal in Boston until after the American Revolution, and Catholics in Ireland would remain disenfranchised into the mid-nineteenth century.

Still, the model that developed was indeed new—a new political theory of government authority. Over the course of centuries—through arguments, crises, persecution, armed conflict, and clashes between Church and state—the West had moved away from a static conception that God granted authority to monarchs, whom we must obey. Christians were not like ancient pagans, submissive to any ruler who claimed the mantle of heaven. Instead, as citizens we took part in a covenant with our rulers. They were bound by the same God who binds us to respect our rights and govern justly. If they did not, we were authorized to replace them.

Given the recent criticisms of John Locke and the American founding, it's worth reflecting on how much this new model departed from what had come before, including from the secularist work of Thomas Hobbes earlier in the seventeenth century. Contrary to what integralists today suggest, there was nothing inevitable about the perversions of law and constitutional principle that led the American legal system to abominations such as *Roe v. Wade* or *Obergefell v. Hodge*. That's the kind of fantasy that armchair political philosophers treasure; they wish to see all the dominos line up perfectly. The reality is that countries with established churches such as England, Sweden, Belgium, and Spain have proven no more resistant to secularist corruption than the United States, with its Natural Law founding.

Instead, we must recognize that secular thinkers willfully hijacked a fundamentally Christian, Humanist system for their own Progressive ends, falsifying in repeated court decisions the real nature of America's founding and the thought of its Founders.[209]

A New Political Order

All the various strands in Christian theory and Anglo-American practice came together and formed something new in America: a political regime based on ordered liberty.

Although the American colonies had been founded with the British crown's permission, for a century or more they essentially governed themselves. As we've seen, colonists shouldered the main burden of self-defense (and often of conquest) against native Americans as well as rival European settlers.

The situation changed in 1763. That's the year the British finally defeated the French in their battle for North America. The British conquest of every French colony removed the great external threat that had justified the presence of British troops in the American colonies. When the French and Indian War ended, the British government attempted to impose centralized rule and British taxes on the colonies. Parliament needed money, and it was eager to flex its muscles. But colonies accustomed to self-governance chafed at Britain's attempt to impose its authority, especially given that Americans had no representation in Parliament.

The American Revolution was a conflict between partisans of liberty and those of top-down authority. This sort of conflict recurs throughout the history of political philosophy. Constitutional attorney Mark W. Smith writes about this in his book *First They Came for the Gun Owners*, noting: "We often (rightly) remember the names and stories of those who fought for freedom. But why did they have to fight? Because many, many people fought against it. Think of the crucial moments when powerful, well-educated, wealthy, and influential people fought on the wrong side—fought against the expansion of freedom, the empowerment of citizens, and the lifting of unjust laws."[210]

Smith includes some examples we have discussed. For example, in 1215, plenty of English barons supported King John and his autocratic rule. We would never have had Magna Carta were it not for the brave barons who stood up to the king, forcing him, as Smith writes, "to offer a written guarantee, binding on his successors, that limited the powers of the monarch."

Or how about the Pilgrims who drew up the Mayflower Compact? Smith writes, "In 1620, the Anglican bishops of England had broad support in persecuting the Puritans at home, imprisoning them for heresy and seizing their churches." But the separatist Puritan Pilgrims had the courage to flee.

They were willing to brave an ocean crossing and survival in an unknown land to form what they called a "Civil Body Politic" committed to enacting "just and equal Laws."

Similarly, Smith points out that in 1628, "thousands of men of power and wealth supported King Charles I's attempts to become an absolute monarch, effectively repealing the rights their ancestors had won with the Magna Carta." But "enough brave members of Parliament stood up to the autocratic Charles to force him to sign the Petition of Right, which restricted his power in important respects and extended key rights from the Magna Carta to ordinary subjects."

The party of liberty and the party of authority faced off again in 1688–89. Although the English Bill of Rights resulted from an event often called the Glorious Revolution, it's worth remembering that many Britons opposed this "glorious" event. As Smith says, "many English lords and their followers bitterly resented the overthrow of absolutist-minded King James II." Of course, it produced a crucial model for both our Declaration of Independence and Bill of Rights.

But that precedent did not make the success of the American Revolution inevitable. The signers of the Declaration of Independence were not being hyperbolic when pledging "our lives, our Fortunes, and our sacred Honor." They took an extraordinary risk in separating from the world's most powerful empire. The risk came not just from British redcoats but also from fellow colonists, many of whom supported King George III and Parliament.

Even after the Americans defeated the British to secure independence, the party of authority did not disappear from these shores. Smith writes: "In 1787, some Americans wanted a much more powerful presidency, even a monarchy. Some privately offered George Washington a throne—but thankfully, the prospect horrified him. More dangerous still: disgruntled, unpaid soldiers of the Continental Army set out to march on the Congress in Philadelphia and impose their own military dictatorship. Again, it took George Washington to talk them out of this plan—which would have set the United States on the same path that South American republics mostly took, with disastrous results for freedom. Instead, representatives of U.S. states created a federal system of government that carefully balanced the powers of each of the three branches of government."

When the loose alliance of states produced by the Articles of Confederation failed, various factions of our Founders looked for a stronger central government. They far exceeded the authority their own states had given them when they drew up a new Constitution with a robust executive branch. Anti-Federalists feared that by strengthening the central government, the newly born United States might slide out of the free tradition and into the authoritarian mold of so many failed republics before it. That is why they insisted on the inclusion of a Bill of Rights as their price for supporting the Constitution's ratification.

Nor did the party of authority vanish with the success of the American founding. The French Revolution slipped

NO SECOND AMENDMENT, NO FIRST

almost immediately from promises of liberty to totalitarianism, with mass conscription, aggressive wars, bloody purges, and religious persecution. The course of the late nineteenth and early twentieth centuries could be described as the resurgence of the authoritarian tradition.

America wasn't immune, and still isn't. Smith writes:

> Every generation has had its share of people who didn't trust their fellow citizens with freedom. Elitists who squinted scornfully at the "commoners." Nativists who didn't trust German or Irish immigrants, because of their language or their religion. Onetime slave owners who wanted to make sure that black Americans couldn't defend their basic rights with firearms.
>
> In the twentieth century, the Progressive movement, led by Woodrow Wilson, took aim at the U.S. Constitution itself in an effort to expand their power to impose social change on recalcitrant free Americans.[211]

And of course, today we contend with enemies of free speech, free religious exercise . . . and the right to bear arms.

The Advantage Americans
Enjoy . . . for Now, at Least

The point of the Bill of Rights was to put strict limits on the powers of the infant government, protecting both states and their citizens from the rise of tyranny. America's Founders had many profound disagreements over the proper powers and structure of the new government. Still, on one subject they were nearly unanimous: the right of ordinary citizens to keep arms and use them in self-defense. They believed citizens should be armed as a perpetual insurance policy against any future tyranny.

A "nuclear option," as we might call it today.

Constitutional scholar Stephen Halbrook documents this overwhelming consensus in his books *The Right to Bear Arms* and *The Founders' Second Amendment*.[212] He notes, for example, that the text of the Second Amendment passed the U.S. House of Representatives with no objections. Halbrook also cites countless statements from state constitutions, along with speeches and letters by state legislators and members of Congress, asserting the centrality of an armed citizenry as the last guarantor of liberty.

Perhaps most notably, James Madison, acknowledged as the "father of the Constitution," wrote in *Federalist* 46 that even if Americans one day faced a tyrannical standing army that served at the behest of the federal government, that army would need to confront "a militia amounting to near half a million of citizens with arms in their hands, officered by men chosen from among themselves, fighting for their common liberties."

Madison added that Americans had an advantage "over the people of almost every other nation"—"the advantage of being armed." By contrast, European governments were "afraid to trust the people with arms," Madison wrote.[213]

Halbrook shows how the only debate over the inclusion of a right to bear arms in the Constitution was over this question: Was such a right so fundamental and obvious that including it explicitly might call its profound, sacred origin into question, making it seem like a privilege granted by the state instead of a right given by God? We can be thankful that the advocates of making the right explicit prevailed.

The Founders didn't just include the right to keep and bear arms in the Bill of Rights; they put it right near the top of the list. The experience of facing, then fighting, the British crown and Parliament had resolved any doubts on the subject.

Remember why the Revolutionary War began in the first place. The Battles of Lexington and Concord broke out because the British marched their soldiers from Boston to Concord to seize the colonists' arms cache there.[214] That is to say, they were trying to disarm the Americans. But militia members— ordinary civilian men armed with privately owned weapons— confronted the British on the Lexington town green.

Citizens' militias proved crucial in the War of Independence. These volunteer militias embodied a profound set of ideas: spontaneous order arising from free citizens. Standing armies directed by monarchs or other powerful executives embodied an opposing set of ideas: the kind of top-down, coercive order that oligarchies and tyrants impose.

For this reason, many of our Founding Fathers were suspicious of standing armies and initially reluctant to found one. They had seen that state militias played a crucial role in fighting the French and Indian War. George Washington himself had led Virginia militiamen who held together and saved the British retreat after the catastrophic defeat of army regulars at the Battle of the Monongahela in 1755. His heroic actions that day helped make him famous.

As Halbrook observes in *That Every Man Be Armed*, Madison, Jefferson, and other champions of independence saw from their study of history that free cities and nations had often succumbed to tyrannical rule imposed by their own military establishments. The Roman Republic had degenerated into an empire when its military ceased to consist of volunteer, short-term citizen soldiers and instead became a professionalized force loyal to its commanders instead of the people.[215]

The Founders protected the right to keep and bear arms not simply because they saw it as the last defense against tyranny. They did so also because they viewed the Second Amendment's protection of private firearms ownership as essential to preserving all the other liberties guaranteed in the Constitution. Several decades after the Second Amendment's ratification, the influential Supreme Court justice and constitutional scholar Joseph Story captured this point when he wrote, "The right of the citizens to keep and bear arms has justly been considered as the palladium of the liberties of a republic."[216]

Or as I've said: No Second Amendment, no First.

CHAPTER 13

THE HUMAN PERSON AND
THE FUTURE OF FREEDOM

My goal in this book has been to show that the Christian view of the person, correctly understood, demands broad rights of self-defense for ordinary citizens—against both illegal violence and the prospect of tyrannical governments. These rights come from God, not from governments. The job of governments is only to mediate and protect the right to armed self-defense. In practice, they too often deprive people of this right.

If you doubt that last claim, remember the long, frightening history of tyrants disarming their people that we reviewed in the opening chapter. That history extends back to ancient times, as David Kopel has shown in an exhaustive study. "When the Philistines conquered the Hebrews, they disarmed them," Kopel writes. "The tyrant Peisistratus of ancient Athens seized political power by disarming the people."[217] And through the centuries, tyrants kept rendering their people defenseless, again and again and again.

Rampant disarmament helped make the twentieth century the bloodiest on record. During that century, governments murdered more than 200 million people—and perhaps many, many more than 200 million.[218] These figures don't count casualties of war.

What did the vast majority of these victims have in common? Their governments had disarmed them. The Ottomans, the Soviets, the Nazis, the Chinese Communists, the Cuban Communists, the Khmer Rouge in Cambodia, and the regime in 1990s Rwanda—these were just some of the modern states that seized weapons from targeted groups, if not all ordinary civilians.[219] Already in the twenty-first century, we've seen Sudan's Islamist regime and Venezuela's authoritarian government take guns from the people.[220]

We must confront these experiences, especially at a time when anti-gun activists in the United States are targeting the right to keep and bear arms. Living according to fantasies quickly ends in tears.

"Terror and Slaughter Return"

Perhaps the greatest political poem in history is Rudyard Kipling's "The Gods of the Copybook Headings." (The term refers to old-fashioned moral maxims of the kind British schoolboys used to copy and recopy so that they might memorize and internalize them.) In the poem, Kipling wryly vindicates the wisdom and "common sense" of our forefathers and the Church Fathers against the grandiose claims and wispy promises of ideologues and innovators:

> We were living in trees when they met us. They
> showed us each in turn
> That Water would certainly wet us, as Fire would
> certainly burn:
> But we found them lacking in Uplift, Vision and
> Breadth of Mind,
> So we left them to teach the Gorillas while we
> followed the March of Mankind.
>
> . . .
>
> With the Hopes that our World is built on they
> were utterly out of touch,
> They denied that the Moon was Stilton; they
> denied she was even Dutch;
> They denied that Wishes were Horses; they denied
> that a Pig had Wings;
> So we worshipped the Gods of the Market Who
> promised these beautiful things.

When the Cambrian measures were forming, They
promised perpetual peace.
They swore, if we gave them our weapons, that the
wars of the tribes would cease.
But when we disarmed They sold us and delivered
us bound to our foe,
And the Gods of the Copybook Headings said:
"Stick to the Devil you know."[221]

The wit Kipling displays here is razor-sharp gallows
humor. He was writing in 1919, as Britain and the rest of
Europe mourned the vast butcher's bill of the First World
War—a conflict started by accident, waged over no principles
of significance, pursued without mercy or limits, that ended
in ruin for every participant. It also sparked the explosion of
Communist revolution that menaced not just Russia but also
Poland, Germany, Hungary, and thus all of Europe.

The brutality, stupidity, and futility of that war convinced
a generation of intellectuals and political influencers to reject
the entire liberal and Christian heritage of the West in favor of
wild new fancies and Utopian dreams of the future.[222]

Indeed, the whole of the twentieth century would see
impatient innovators kick aside the tenets of Natural Law,
Christian morality, the dignity of man, and the rights of the
individual. They claimed that their new presentations of often
ancient heresies were the conclusions of "research," "progress,"
and "science." The "old-fashioned" values hadn't stopped
Europe from stumbling into World War I, the young poets

and demagogues sneered. Ezra Pound wrote savagely in "Hugh Selwyn Mauberley":

There died a myriad,

And of the best, among them,

For an old bitch gone in the teeth,

For a botched civilization.[223]

The new and "hopeful" programs that ideological pilgrims like Pound would embrace had names like eugenics, fascism, communism, National Socialism, free love, and feminism. They would rack up their own butcher's bill that exceeded by 150 million the losses of World War I. Here I'm not including the 1.6 billion abortions committed (as of this writing) since 1980,[224] but that number must not be forgotten when we speak of the blood spilled thanks to ideologies that reject the Christian worldview.

Kipling warned of such damage in the conclusion to his poem:

And that after this is accomplished, and the brave
new world begins
When all men are paid for existing and no man
must pay for his sins,

As surely as Water will wet us, as surely as Fire will
burn,
The Gods of the Copybook Headings with terror
and slaughter return!

A lifetime of deferring to the self-styled elites in this
country has taught otherwise rational, intelligent people to
filter out obvious truths in favor of "nuanced," "sophisticated"
lies or manifest nonsense. They learn the slogans required for
social acceptance and promotion.

It takes a college education, maybe even a master's degree,
to really convince oneself that there are actually forty-seven
genders instead of two. Likewise, to treasure the idea that
"real Marxism has never been tried." Could we say the same of
fascism, then? Why not?

It takes years of training in intellectual conformism to
condition our God-given minds to operate that badly and
suppress such blatant questions. But millions of Americans
have put in the effort, and we can see the results in our spiraling
economy, broken borders, and corrupting, chaotic schools.

Scapegoats Need Gun Rights
More Than Anyone Else

Let me bluntly state one brutally obvious truth that far
too many Americans have learned to ignore: In a society where
guns are forbidden to private citizens, the least popular groups
are those most endangered. This is especially true if the govern-

ment isn't committed to protecting those friendless minorities (as few governments historically are, over the long haul—eventually there comes a Pharaoh who knew not Joseph).

This truth was obvious in America in the backlash after Reconstruction, when local and state governments in the South moved to reimpose white supremacy. Some of the first gun-control laws in America were passed as Jim Crow measures, to strip free blacks of the power to defend themselves against vigilantes and the Ku Klux Klan. In 1892, journalist and activist Ida B. Wells, who had been born into slavery, published a searing exposé of lynchings, *Southern Horrors*. In it, Wells wrote that the few recent instances when black men escaped lynchings occurred when they had guns and used them in self-defense. Wells concluded, "The lesson this teaches and which every Afro-American should ponder well, is that a Winchester rifle should have a place of honor in every black home, and it should be used for that protection which the law refuses to give."[225]

Alas, many state and local governments continued to deny black Americans their God-given right to self-defense. That left them vulnerable not only to lynchings but also to white-led race riots like the one that devastated Tulsa, Oklahoma, in 1921. Over an eighteen-hour period, a white mob attacked a prosperous African-American neighborhood that Booker T. Washington called the "Black Wall Street." The New York Times summed up the horrifying damage: "35 blocks burned to the ground; as many as 300 dead; hundreds injured; 8,000 to 10,000 left homeless; more than 1,470 homes burned or looted; and eventually, 6,000 detained in internment camps."[226]

As modern American culture becomes inexorably more hostile to orthodox Christianity, with its "outdated" sexual morals and links to our nation's demonized past, that means gun control will be especially dangerous for Christians. This isn't a deduction but a grim observation.

Recall that in 2022, after news broke that the Supreme Court would overturn *Roe v. Wade*, dozens of church-linked crisis pregnancy centers and pro-life groups were vandalized or attacked.[227] The Biden administration did nothing, not even condemning the incidents.[228] But the same administration moved aggressively to suppress "misgendering" of "trans" service members in the U.S. military.[229] Some vulnerable groups are more equal than others.

Nobody can really trust the modern secular state with a monopoly of violence. But unpopular minorities can trust it least of all. The Christians of the Middle East learned this lesson in an especially bitter fashion over the past two decades.

Let us consider the fates of two relatively similar communities of Christians. Each has been present in the Middle East since the age of the Apostles. Each endured centuries of Arab and then Ottoman occupation. I'm referring to the Syriac Christians of Syria and the Chaldean and Assyrian Christians of Iraq. As of September 11, 2001, each group was in a similar situation: a small, unpopular minority, subject to suspicion and envy on the part of Muslim majorities. Each had been beaten down by centuries of Muslim occupation and learned to depend on a secular, Baathist dictatorship for protection from jihad violence. There were no other options.

Then came the U.S. invasion of Iraq in 2003. The United States destroyed the regime of Saddam Hussein, dissolved the Baathist party, and unleashed the long-simmering forces of interreligious hatred. The once-dominant Sunni minority battled the long-suppressed Shiite majority, and both battled the comparatively secular Sunni Kurds. The one group that all the others saw no reason to protect, and that many scapegoated for the invasion by American "crusaders," were the helpless local Christians.

The U.S. government under both George W. Bush and Barack Obama pursued the same policy toward the persecution of Christians: they ignored it. Even though the U.S. invasion had unleashed that violence, and resentment of Americans encouraged it, neither administration showed any initiative in protecting Christians from religious violence.[230]

Worse, the provisional government the United States had installed adopted a policy of strict gun control for private citizens. Of course, Muslim militias ignored such laws completely. But the laws kept Iraqi Christians from obtaining the firearms that might have helped them resist persecution.

The result was miserable and predictable. Iraq had an estimated 1.5 million Christians before the U.S. invasion in 2003. By 2021, church officials estimated that just a few hundred thousand remained there. Why had the population plummeted? Because militant Islamists sweeping Iraq had butchered Christians, forcing others to flee the country.

Particularly chilling is the story of ISIS's conquest of Mosul in 2014. In only a few hours, a few hundred armed ISIS militants took over a city of 1.6 million people, with many thousands of Christians. ISI swept across the Nineveh Plains in northern Iraq, seizing many other towns and villages.

The Associated Press reported:

> Thousands of Christians found themselves fleeing once again the militants' advance, taking refuge in Iraq's northern Kurdish region or leaving the country. Over the next few years, the extremists killed thousands of Iraqi civilians from a variety of religions. They also destroyed buildings and ruined historical and culturally significant structures they considered contrary to their interpretation of Islam. Militants from the Islamic State group demolished religious and historic sites, including monasteries, mosques, tombs, shrines and churches in Syria and Iraq.[231]

I heard firsthand reports of Iraqi Christians huddled in unheated shipping containers—since Islamists controlled even the refugee camps the United Nations ran. U.S. troops looked on and did nothing.

"Mission Accomplished," indeed.

Today, the remaining Christians in the Nineveh Plains are struggling with Iraq's Shiite-dominated government for the right to obtain weapons to protect themselves against the next collapse of order.[232] The Christian community in the country, which endured more than a thousand years of Muslim occupation, could not survive ten years of American-style gun control.

The story of Christians in Syria provides an illuminating and uplifting contrast.

As if Providence had arranged for a kind of controlled experiment, in neighboring Syria, a similar group of Christians faced a parallel situation. Long protected by the tyrannical but secular Assad regime, Christians in Syria faced the prospect of the same chaos hitting them. Encouraged by the "Arab Spring" rhetoric of reckless American statesmen, Islamist rebels were trying to replace Assad's government with a fundamentalist Muslim regime linked to al-Qaeda.

American liberals and neoconservatives actively tried to help them. In 2016, every Republican presidential candidate apart from Rand Paul, Ted Cruz, and Donald Trump supported the U.S. shooting down Russian planes to help these Islamists take power—where they surely would have repeated the bloody purges of Christians we'd seen in Iraq.

But Trump won the nomination and then the presidency. He didn't play nuclear chicken with Russia to help those "moderate rebels" linked to al-Qaeda come to power. Instead, he gave aid to secular, nationalist Kurdish rebels in Syria. And here is where things got interesting.

One group of Syrian Christians clung to protection from the embattled Assad regime, which patrolled them and controlled them. They are still physically safe today, though far from free. (The secret police monitor communications among the clergy and infiltrate their churches.) Their fragile condition of dhimmitude under a grudgingly tolerant government suggests the fate of American Christians in the very near future.

Another group of Christians in Syria took a much riskier road, but one with more hope. They aligned with the Kurdish rebels and genuine Arab moderates, joining forces with their militias. They armed and trained themselves, and helped the Kurds fight a three-front war against Islamist jihadists, the forces of ISIS, and the Syrian government army, which is supported by Vladimir Putin's Russia. With Kurds taking the lead, this coalition has carved out a region in northeastern Syria that is genuinely democratic, religiously tolerant, and free.

In the Autonomous Administration of North and East Syria (AANES), unlike any other part of the Middle East except for Israel, Christians are free to evangelize their faith. Muslims are free to practice their own or join another. There is no sharia law, no secret police, no honor killing, and no dungeons where dissidents are tortured. Christians don't shiver in shipping containers or beg for admission to refugee camps. They govern their own small communities and fight in their own militias.

What is more, in 2017, with active assistance from the United States, the Syrian Democratic Forces that fight for AANES attacked the armies of ISIS. In just a few months they conquered the last of ISIS's territory, wiping its so-called caliphate off the face of the earth. Now even the regime in Damascus must reluctantly deal with AANES as a neighbor, and its diverse communities are safe for the near future.[233]

That is the difference that Christians and others subject to persecution can make when they are granted their fundamental right of self-defense. Indeed, it's what free citizens can accomplish in rebuking tyranny anywhere in the world. The Christians in many other troubled countries such as Nigeria are currently crippled by well-intentioned, profoundly foolish laws that keep them helpless in the face of jihadi violence. Christians in safe countries shouldn't be blandly calling for "an end to the violence," but actively helping these persecuted believers to arm themselves.

Maybe we can also take a deeper lesson. To protect their community, Christians in Syria had to choose between meekly seeking protection from a hostile secular regime and joining forces with populist and nationalist allies who might not share their faith.

We face a similar choice here in America.

The Only Way Forward

Throughout this book, I've tried to articulate the correct way for Christians to form their consciences as citizens in a modern, post-Christian context. As it draws to a close—after we have surveyed thousands of years of history, both Testaments of scripture, the growth of authoritative Church tradition, and the profound political changes the Christian view of the person brought to the West—is there a simple message to sum it all up?

The answer is yes. The message is:

Freedom in the sense we take for granted, based on individual rights, arose only in the West, and only the Christian West. That's not an accident. The Christian roots of our regime of ordered liberty are not a primitive "phase" that we can grow out of. No, the Biblical view of the person is the soil where liberty sprouted. It feeds our liberty, keeping it alive. Yank the tree out of the soil and the leaves will stay green for a while, but it's as good as dead already. That's the stage where we are today, still staring at the leaves as the tree gasps for its life. It never "outgrows" its need for water and nutrients.

So how can any principled person think about politics in the tradition of our Christian ancestors, the ones who created this system of freedom, when considering complex moral issues? The only sane way is first to consider the human person as revealed to us by God in both Testaments and then to think through the implications of that human dignity for life in society.

EPILOGUE

Obituary, Jacob "Superman" Gardner, November 14, 1981 – September 20, 2020

On November 14, 1981, Jake Gardner was born in El Paso, Texas. He was bright-eyed, sharp, kind, funny, and inquisitive as a child. They were all aspects of his personality that followed him into adulthood. He attended the Northeast Christian Academy in El Paso from kindergarten to seventh grade. His childhood in Texas was spent shopping with his mother, enjoying her beef brisket and other wonderful dishes, watching movies with his dad, reading comic books with his younger brother, and attending church with his grandmother …

In November 2000 Jake enlisted in the United States Marine Corps Infantry. Years later, while reminiscing on that time in his life, he said, "It takes a special type of person who is willing to take a bullet for his country." When Jake showed up to boot camp, he weighed about 140 lbs. As his drill instructors soon found out, most of that weight was heart. While many wise recruits know that keeping a low profile during boot camp is a good policy, that was not the tactic Jake chose to employ. A few weeks before he shipped out to MCRD (Marine Corps Recruiting Depot?) San Diego Jake had gotten a tattoo. As the platoon stood online shirtless for the first time his drill instructors' eyes began to bulge out of their heads. His tattoo covered his chest, it was a full-size full color Superman emblem. From that moment on his nickname, "Superman," was born.

After completing the School of Infantry, and the Light Armored Vehicle crewman course, Jake was sent to 2nd Light Armored Reconnaissance (LAR) Battalion in Camp Lejeune, North Carolina. He was first assigned to the Weapons Company Mortar Platoon, then to Bravo Company. On March 20, 2003 the ground war in Iraq began. The Marines of 2nd LAR served as the tip of the spear of the RCT 1 invasion force. The unit received the Presidential Unit Citation for completing the longest sequence of coordinated overland attacks in Marine Corps history. While he served bravely in combat, many of his fellow Marines recall the way he used his humor to keep morale high even during the most tense of situations. After four months of continuous combat operations Jake returned to Camp Lejeune. His break from combat was short lived. He deployed as part of a quick reaction force to Haiti in February of 2004. It was in Haiti that Jake earned his second combat action ribbon.

Jake Gardner was honorably discharged in November, 2004. He left the Marines with a long list of brothers in arms. Some he kept in contact with until his death, and some had already made the ultimate sacrifice whose memories he cherished until they met at the gates of heaven.

After the Military, Jake enrolled at Metro Community college in Omaha, before moving to Arcata, California to attend Humboldt State University. It was there on the beaches of the redwood coast that Jake found some peace. It was much needed, and well deserved after his experiences overseas. In 2009, he returned back to Omaha with his trusty Czech Shepherd service dog Lebron, named after Jake's favorite basketball player. Lebron accompanied Jake everywhere, including five NBA final's games.

An aspiring entrepreneur, he started his first business in 2009. It was a lawn care business called Amerigreen. In 2010 he started bartending, and in 2011 he opened his first bar, the Hive lounge. Jake didn't look at bar ownership the same way as many other owners in the industry. Instead of just serving drinks, Jake strove to throw the best party he could every night. The Hive hosted Omaha's first reggae night, and years later he added salsa dance night as well.

In 2014 he met a woman that became the love of his life. They travelled, laughed, took pictures, watched movies, walked their dogs, and cared dearly for one another until his end and beyond.

His business thrived, when asked what the secret to his success was, he responded simply. "Make every woman that walks through the door feel safe, and only play music that people want to dance to."

When the scourge of the Coronavirus took hold of the country, Jake's business ground to a halt. On May 30, 2020 he was busy preparing for his business to reopen the following week. Tragically, that night violent rioters committed assaults and property damage in downtown Omaha. Jake's plan was simple: protect his business from being burned, pull the fire alarm and call the police when the windows were broken. The windows were broken, and Jake called the police and pulled the fire alarm. After the crowd of destructive rioters cleared the street, Jake and his father went out on the sidewalk to survey the damage.

Unfortunately, the property damage was not enough to appease the violent mob, and many rioters returned to find more targets of opportunity. More windows began to be broken and Jake's father told the rioters responsible to leave. Then the surveillance video shows his father was violently attacked. Jake did not see the assault on his father, but ran up the street and positioned himself in between the advancing violent mob and his downed father. For over 50 feet, Jake walked backwards trying to deescalate the situation.

In the final moments of the altercation Jake was tackled by multiple assailants. With his back on the concrete, as a last resort, he discharged one warning shot in the air with the pistol he was legally allowed to possess in that situation under Nebraska state Law. Jake's original attackers fled, and Jake rolled over on his hands and knees to try to get up. At that moment another assailant jumped on Jake's back and put him in a rear naked choke. It was a technique designed to try to kill him.

The incident marked the third time that evening that Jake's current assailant had attacked the business. Jake's final assailant was a violent career criminal, who had already been convicted of an armed home invasion, and the beating of a pregnant woman, his own child's mother. The assailant was trying to choke Jake to death. Jake can be heard pleading with his assailant on the video evidence, "Get off me, get off me, please get off me." To save his own life, Jake Gardner was forced to reach over his shoulder, then shoot and kill his attacker.

The following day, Omaha District Attorney Don Klein had a press conference where he showed the video exonerating Jake Gardner of any wrongdoing, and announced Jake would not be charged. Sadly, after 36 days of protests outside his house the D.A. caved to the will of the mob, and appointed Fred Franklin as a special prosecutor. Fred Franklin convened a grand jury, then engaged in the falsifying of evidence and other unlawful conduct. Franklin's motives are undoubtedly nefarious, but according to a US attorney that worked with Franklin one stands out, greed.

By trying a man whom Franklin knew to be innocent, it is speculated that he may have been hoping to be involved in a high-profile case and make money selling a book about it. Jake faced possible terms of 94 years in prison for unjust charges. This was for having the courage to defend his own life from a violent multiple felon who was actively trying to choke him to death, all of which was captured on high resolution video. As Jake once remarked, "It's hard to know what someone looks like when they jump on your back in the middle of the night and try to choke you to death."

After the corrupt decision of the grand jury based on falsified evidence was revealed, Jake lost all hope in the legal system and tragically ended his own life on September 20, 2020. Jake Gardner was laid to rest among other heroes of this great nation in Arlington, Virginia, with full military honors.

Those who knew and loved Jake are people that represent different races, cultures, and creeds. All will remember Jake's smile, his character, his dedication to defend the Constitution, his wit, his intellect, and his willingness to help those in need. He was a man that fought valiantly against terrorism and violent extremism in Iraq, Haiti, and Omaha. He was, truly, a Superman. We pray that he has found eternal peace among the sound of lapping waves on heaven's beach.

Reprinted by permission of the author, who asked that his own name not be used.

ABOUT THE AUTHOR

J ohn Zmirak graduated from Yale in 1986 with a Bachelors degree in Religion and Literature, and from Louisiana State University in 1996 with a Ph.D. in English literature. He is author, co-author, or editor of 12 other books, including *The Bad Catholic's Guide to the Seven Deadly Sins*, *The Politically Incorrect Guide to Immigration*, *The Grand Inquisitor*, and *The Race to Save Our Century*. He is Senior Editor at The Stream (Stream.org).

ENDNOTES

1 "New Mexico Governor Suspends Gun Rights in Albuquerque for "Public Health Emergency," Jonathanturley.org, https://jonathanturley.org/2023/09/09/new-mexico-governor-suspends-gun-rights-in-albuquerque-for-public-health-emergency/

2 "New Mexico sheriff REFUSES to enforce governor's ban on carrying guns, says it's unconstitutional," Post-Millennial, September 9, 2023, https://thepostmillennial.com/new-mexico-sheriff-refuses-to-enforce-governors-ban-on-carrying-guns-says-its-unconstitutional

3 Sarah Volpenhein, "Kyle Rittenhouse Was Charged with Intentional and Reckless Homicide in Kenosha Protest Shootings," *Milwaukee Journal Sentinel*, August 27, 2020, https://www.jsonline.com/story/news/2020/08/26/kyle-rittenhouse-charged-kenosha-protest-shootings-militia/5634532002/.

4 Among many other examples, see Jessica Chasmar, "Psaki Slams 'Vigilantes' with 'Assault Weapons' After Saying She Can't Comment on Rittenhouse Trial," Fox News, November 15, 2021, https://www.foxnews.com/politics/psaki-vigilantes-assault-weapons-rittenhouse-trial; Charles M. Blow, "Rittenhouse and the Right's White Vigilante Heroes," *New York Times*, November 19, 2021, https://www.nytimes.com/2021/11/19/opinion/kyle-rittenhouse-not-guilty-vigilantes.html; Paige Williams, "Kyle Rittenhouse, American Vigilante," New Yorker, June 28, 2021, https://www.newyorker.com/magazine/2021/07/05/kyle-rittenhouse-american-vigilante; Congresswoman Ayanna Pressley (D-MA), Twitter, August 26, 2020, https://twitter.com/AyannaPressley/status/1298780540431224832?ref_src=twsrc ("white supremacist domestic terrorist"); Brittany Bernstein, "Psaki Defends Biden Campaign Video Labeling Rittenhouse 'White Supremacist,'" *National Review*, November 23, 2021, https://www.nationalreview.com/news/psaki-on-biden-calling-rittenhouse-a-white-supremacist-the-president-believes-in-condemning-hatred-divison-violence/; Erin Snodgrass and Michelle Mark, "Kyle Rittenhouse Didn't Illegally Bring a Gun Across State Lines and 5 Other Myths Surrounding the Trial Debunked," *Insider*, November 19, 2021, https://www.insider.com/6-myths-surrounding-the-kyle-rittenhouse-trial-debunked-2021-11.

5 "A Look Back at How the Kyle Rittenhouse Shooting Unfolded in Kenosha," NBC 5 Chicago, November 1, 2021, https://www.nbcchicago.com/news/local/a-look-back-at-how-the-kyle-rittenhouse-shooting-unfolded-in-kenosha/2665888/; Christina Maxouris, "More Than a Dozen Video Clips Were Played During Kyle Rittenhouse's Trial Last Week. Here's What They Showed," CNN, November 8, 2021, https://www.cnn.com/2021/11/07/us/kyle-rittenhouse-trial-what-video-evidence-shows/index.html.

6 Michael Tarm, Scott Bauer, and Amy Forliti, "Jury Finds Rittenhouse Not Guilty in Kenosha Shootings," Associated Press, November 19, 2021, https://apnews.com/article/jury-finds-kyle-rittenhouse-not-guilty-in-kenosha-shootings-27f812ba532d65c-044617483c915e4de.

7 Brad Polumbo, "George Floyd Riots Caused Record-Setting $2 Billion in Damage, New Report Says. Here's Why the True Cost Is Even Higher," Foundation for Economic Education, September 16, 2020, https://fee.org/articles/george-floyd-riots-caused-record-setting-2-billion-in-damage-new-report-says-here-s-why-the-true-cost-is-even-higher/.

8 Lois Beckett, "At Least 25 Americans Were killed During Protests and Political Unrest in 2020," *The Guardian* (UK), October 31, 2020, https://www.theguardian.com/world/2020/oct/31/americans-killed-protests-political-unrest-acled .

9 Ann Coulter, "Ann Coulter: Innocent Uuntil Proven Trump Supporter," *Townhall*, September 23, 2020, https://townhall.com/columnists/anncoulter/2020/09/23/innocent-until-proven-trump-supporter-n2576797.

10 Ben Kesslen, "Nebraska Bar Owner Charged in Killing of Black Man During George Floyd Protests Dies by Suicide," NBC News, September 21, 2020, https://www.nbcnews.com/news/us-news/nebraska-bar-owner-charged-killing-black-man-during-george-floyd-n1240596.

11 Coulter, "Innocent Until Proven Trump Supporter."

12 Kara Eastman, Twitter, May 31, 2020, https://twitter.com/_karaeastman/status/1267099716359241735.

13 See Michelle Bandur, "'He Lost His Faith in the Justice System': Jake Gardner's Best Friend Speaks About His Suicide," KETV 7 Omaha, October 5, 2020, https://www.ketv.com/article/he-lost-his-faith-in-the-justice-system-jake-gardners-best-friend-speaks-about-his-suicide/34211653#; Coulter, "Innocent Until Proven Trump Supporter."

14 Margery A. Beck and Josh Funk, "Prosecutor to Call for Grand Jury Review of Protest Killing," Associated Press, June 3, 2020, https://apnews.com/article/ded4eef9f4dc05c6ae-feebc19d554830.

15 "Don Kleine Stands by His Decision Not to Charge Jake Gardner," KMTV 3 News Now, September 23, 2020, https://www.3newsnow.com/news/local-news/don-kleine-and-gardners-lawyers-comment-on-prosecutors-briefing.

16 Khaleda Rahman, "Jake Gardner, Bar Owner Indicted in Killing of Black Protester, Dies by Suicide," *Newsweek*, September 21, 2020, https://www.newsweek.com/jake-gardner-james-scurlock-bar-owner-indicted-killing-black-protester-suicide-1533192.

17 "Property Owner Says Hive, Gatsby Will Not Be Allowed to Reopen," KETV 7 Omaha, June 2, 2020, https://www.ketv.com/article/property-owner-says-hive-gatsby-will-not-be-allowed-to-reopen/32746123.

18 Teia Goodwin, "Property Owner Where Black Protester Was Killed Issues Statement," Fox 42 KPTM, June 3, 2020, https://fox42kptm.com/news/local/property-owner-where-black-protester-was-killed-issues-statement.

19 Mia Cathell, "Friend of Jake Gardner Reveals His Last Messages Before His Suicide, Calls Out Left-Wing Mob Who Doxxed and Defamed Him," *Post Millennial*, September 21, 2020, https://thepostmillennial.com/exclusive-jake-gardners-friend-speaks-out

20 Senator Megan Hunt, Twitter, September 20, 2020, https://twitter.com/nebraskamegan/status/1307882695687581697.

21 Lindsay Kornick, "Biden Blasted for Mocking 'Brave' Second Amendment Defenders: 'You Need an F-15' to Fight America, Not a Gun," Fox News, August 30, 2022, https://www.foxnews.com/media/biden-blasted-mocking-brave-second-amendment-defenders-you-need-f-15-fight-america-not-gun.

22 See, e.g., "Remarks by President Biden After Marine One Arrival," White House, May 30, 2022, https://www.whitehouse.gov/briefing-room/speeches-remarks/2022/05/30/remarks-by-president-biden-after-marine-one-arrival-10/; Sinéad Baker, "Biden Mocked Gun-Rights Advocates Who Say They Need Assault Weapons to Fight the Government: 'You Need F-15s and Maybe Some Nuclear Weapons,'" *Business Insider*, June 24, 2021, https://www.businessinsider.com/biden-mocks-gun-right-advocates-who-say-assault-weapons-needed-fight-government-2021-6; David Harsanyi, "Joe Biden's Incoherent Second Amendment Rant," *National Review*, February 10, 2020, https://www.nationalreview.com/2020/02/joe-biden-gun-rights-doesnt-understand-second-amendment/.

23David B. Kopel, Paul Gallant, and Joanne D. Eisen, "Is Resisting Genocide a Human Right?" *Notre Dame Law Review* 81, no. 4 (2006), https://scholarship.law.nd.edu/cgi/viewcontent.cgi?article=1347&context=ndlr.

24 Nelson Lund, "The Second Amendment, Political Liberty, and the Right to Self-Preservation," *Alabama Law Review* 39 (1987), https://heinonline.org/HOL/LandingPage?handle=hein.journals/bamalr39&div=9&id=&page=.

25 Hollie McKay, "Venezuelans Regret Gun Ban, 'A Declaration of War Against an Unarmed Population,'" Fox News, December 14, 2018, https://www.foxnews.com/world/venezuelans-regret-gun-prohibition-we-could-have-defended-ourselves.

26 David B. Kopel, "Guns Kill People, and Tyrants with Gun Monopolies Kill the Most," *Gonzaga Journal of International Law* 25, no. 1 (Fall 2021), https://gjil.scholasticahq.com/article/40361-guns-kill-people-and-tyrants-with-gun-monopolies-kill-the-most; Kopel, Gallant, and Eisen, "Is Resisting Genocide a Human Right?"

27 Austin Prochko, "Armed Populace Serves as Check on Government Overreach," *Washington Times*, June 20, 2022, https://www.washingtontimes.com/news/2022/jun/20/armed-populace-serves-as-check-on-government-overr/.

28 Kopel, "Guns Kill People, and Tyrants with Gun Monopolies Kill the Most."

29 "Declaration of the Rights of the Laboring and Exploited People," Central Executive Committee, January 16, 1918, https://soviethistory.msu.edu/1917-2/workers-organization/workers-organization-texts/7149-2/.

30 "Decree on the Surrender of Weapons." Council of People's Commissars, December 10, 1918, http://museumreforms.ru/node/13766.

31 Yuri M. Zhukov, "Taking Away the Guns: Forcible Disarmament and Rebellion," *Journal of Peace Research* 53, no. 2 (March 2016), https://scholar.harvard.edu/files/zhukov/files/2015_zhukov_jpr_preprint.pdf; Robert Conquest, *The Harvest of Sorrow: Soviet Collectivization and the Terror-Famine* (New York: Oxford University Press, 1986), 154.

32 Aleksandr Solzhenitsyn, *The Gulag Archipelago, 1918–1956: An Experiment in Literary Investigation*, I–II (Glasgow: Collins/Fontana, 1974), 13.

33 Yaron Steinbuch, "Black Lives Matter co-founder describes herself as 'trained Marxist,'" *New York Post*, June 25, 2020, https://nypost.com/2020/06/25/blm-co-founder-describes-herself-as-trained-marxist/

34 A "verst" is a Russian unit of measure equivalent to about two-thirds of a mile.

35 Vladimir Ilyich Lenin, "Telegram to Comrades Kuraev, Bosh, Minkin, and Other Penza Communists," Marxists Internet Archive, https://www.marxists.org/archive/lenin/works/1918/aug/11c.htm.

36 Samuel Gregg, "The Most Dangerous Socialist in History," *The Stream*, July 25, 2016, https://stream.org/dangerous-marxist/.

37 "AG Paxton Sues Biden Administration for Silencing Parents, Labeling Them "Terrorists," Office of the Attorney General, State of Texas, March 4, 2022, https://www.texasattorneygeneral.gov/news/releases/ag-paxton-sues-biden-administration-silencing-parents-labeling-them-terrorists

38 Evan Thomas, "Michelle Obama's 'Proud' Remarks," Newsweek, March 12, 2008, https://www.newsweek.com/michelle-obamas-proud-remarks-83559.

39 "The Surveillance and Political Spying Operations Highlighted by John Durham Are the Tip of the Iceberg," The Last Refuge, February 12, 2022, https://theconservativetreehouse.com/blog/2022/02/12/the-surveillance-and-political-spying-operations-highlighted-by-john-durham-are-the-tip-of-the-iceberg/.

40 John Zmirak, "The War on Terror," in *American Conservatism: An Encyclopedia* (Wilmington, DE: ISI Books, 2006).

41 Sarah Taylor, "Boulder mass killing suspect who reportedly criticized Trump for his immigration stance was 'previously known' by FBI: Report," *The Blaze*, March 24, 2021, https://www.theblaze.com/news/boulder-mass-killing-suspect-was-previously-known-by-fbi-report.

42 Charles Creitz, "Tucker Confronts NJ Gov Over Lockdown Measures: 'I Wasn't Thinking of the Bill of Rights When We Did This,'" Fox News, April 15, 2020, https://www.foxnews.com/media/tucker-carlson-phil-murphy-bill-of-rights.

43 John Gage, "De Blasio Threatens to Permanently Close Places of Worship That Resist Shutdown Order," *Washington Examiner*, March 29, 2020, https://www.washingtonexaminer.com/news/de-blasio-threatens-to-permanently-close-places-of-worship-that-resist-shutdown-order.

44 Tim Carpenter, "Influx of Texas, Oklahoma residents seeking an abortion drives up Kansas total in 2020," Kansas Reflector, June 1, 2021, https://kansasreflector.com/2021/06/01/influx-of-texas-oklahoma-residents-seeking-an-abortion-drives-up-kansas-total-in-2020/

45 Elizabeth Cohen, John Bonifield, and Justin Lape, "'Something Has to Be Done': After Decades of Near-Silence from the CDC, the Agency's Director Is Speaking Up About Gun Violence," CNN, August 28, 2021, https://www.cnn.com/2021/08/27/health/cdc-gun-research-walensky/index.html.

46 "What It Would take to Treat Gun Violence as a Public Health Crisis," All Things Considered, NPR, February 5, 2022, https://www.npr.org/2022/02/05/1078546542/what-it-would-take-to-treat-gun-violence-as-a-public-health-crisis.

47 Peter Nicholas, "Biden Says He'll Renew Push for Assault Weapons Ban Following Spate of Mass Shootings," NBC News, November 24, 2022, https://www.cnbc.com/2022/11/24/biden-says-hell-renew-push-for-assault-weapons-ban.html.

48 Lindsay Kornick, "Biden Blasted for Mocking 'Brave' Second Amendment Defenders: 'You Need an F-15' to Fight America, Not a Gun," Fox News, August 30, 2022, https://www.foxnews.com/media/biden-blasted-mocking-brave-second-amendment-defenders-you-need-f-15-fight-america-not-gun; "Remarks by President Biden After Marine One Arrival," White House, May 30, 2022, https://www.whitehouse.gov/briefing-room/speeches-remarks/2022/05/30/remarks-by-president-biden-after-marine-one-arrival-10/; Sinéad Baker, "Biden Mocked Gun-Rights Advocates Who Say They Need Assault Weapons to Fight the Government: 'You Need F-15s and Maybe Some Nuclear Weapons,'" *Business Insider,* June 24, 2021, https://www.businessinsider.com/biden-mocks-gun-right-advocates-who-say-assault-weapons-needed-fight-government-2021-6; David Harsanyi, "Joe Biden's Incoherent Second Amendment Rant," *National Review,* February 10, 2020, https://www.nationalreview.com/2020/02/joe-biden-gun-rights-doesnt-understand-second-amendment/.

49 "Gun Violence Must End Now," The National Council of Churches, August 5, 2019. https://nationalcouncilofchurches.us/gun-violence-must-end-now/,

50 "President of United States Conference of Catholic Bishops and the Chairman of the USCCB's Committee on Domestic Justice Issued a Statement After a Tragic Shooting in Dayton, Ohio," U.S. Conference of Catholic Bishops, August 4, 2019. http://www.usccb.org/news/2019/19-143.cfm.

51 "Planned Parenthood Admits to U.S. Supreme Court that CMP's Undercover Videos Are True," Center for Medical Progress, August 23, 2023, https://www.centerformedicalprogress.org/2023/08/breaking-planned-parenthood-admits-to-u-s-supreme-court-that-cmps-undercover-videos-are-true/

52 Blase Cupich, "Planned Parenthood and the Muted Humanity of the Unborn Child," Chicago Tribune, August 3, 2015. https://www.chicagotribune.com/opinion/commentary/ct-blase-cupich-abortion-planned-parenthood-perspec-0804-20150803-story.html.

53 https://www.newyorker.com/news/on-religion/god-guns-and-country-the-evangelical-fight-over-firearms

54 "Statement on Weekend's Pair of Assault Weapons Mass Murders," Heeding God's Call to End Gun Violence, August 5, 2019. https://static1.squarespace.com/static/5bca47eee4afe972b2b52249/t/5d49ab034dbeb60001c42917/1565108996271/Statement%2C+Heeding%2C+Pair+of+Assault+Weapons+Mass+Shootings%2C+BMiller%2C+8-5-19.pdf

55 John Gravino, *Confronting the Pope of Suspicion: Special 2021 Edition* (2019, 2021), Chapter 1 ff.

56 Dr. William Coulson & Dr. William Marra, "The Story of a Repentant Psychologist," EWTN, https://www.ewtn.com/catholicism/library/story-of-a-repentant-psychologist-11932 . See also William Kilpatrick, *Psychological Seduction*, (Nashville, TN: Nelsonword Publishing, 1983).

57 Eugene F. Diamond, "Linacre Institute Symposium, The Clerical Sex Abuse Crisis: Introduction," *The Linacre Quarterly*, Vol. IX, 3: https://epublications.marquette.edu/lnq/vol69/iss3/1

See also Philip Lawler, *The Faithful Departed*, (New York, N.Y.: Encounter Books, 2010).

58 William Dalrymple, *Admirable Evasions: How Psychology Undermines Morality*, (New York, N.Y.: Encounter Books, 2020).

59 Jennifer Roback Morse, *The Sexual State*, (Gastonia, N.C., TAN Books, 2018).

60 "Ex-pope says sexual revolution led to abuse crisis, sparking debate," Philip Pullela, Reuters, April 11, 2019, https://www.reuters.com/article/us-pope-abuse-benedict/ex-pope-says-sexual-revolution-led-to-abuse-crisis-sparking-debate-idUSKCN1RN0WI

61 https://www.songlyrics.com/west-side-story/gee-officer-krupke-lyrics/

62 Julie Kelly, *January 6: How Democrats Used the Capitol Protest to Launch a War on Terror Against the Political Right*, (New York, N.Y.: Bombardier Books, 2021).

63 Dana Loesch, "Why Red Flag Laws Are Not a Good Solution to Mass Shootings," *The Federalist*, August 6, 2019. https://thefederalist.com/2019/08/06/red-flag-laws-not-good-solution-mass-shootings/.

64 "Colorado's guidance to police on the red flag law doesn't include what to do if someone won't give up their guns," Jesse Paul, *Colorado Sun*, December 4, 2019, https://coloradosun.com/2019/12/04/colorado-red-flag-law-policies-gun-seizures/

65 "Colorado's New 'Red Flag' Law Illustrates the Pitfalls of Disarming People Based on Their Future Behavior," Jacob Sullum, Reason, April 29, 2019, https://reason.com/2019/04/29/colorados-new-red-flag-law-illustrates-the-pitfalls-of-disarming-people-based-on-their-future-behavior/

66 *The Law* (Auburn, Alabama, Ludwig von Mises Institute, 2007), p. 23.

67 *McDonald v. Chicago*, 561 U.S. 742 (2010), https://supreme.justia.com/cases/federal/us/561/742/

68 Charles Creitz, "Nicholas Sandmann Reaches Settlement with NBC in Covington Catholic High School Controversy," Fox News, December 17, 2021, https://www.foxnews.com/media/nicholas-sandmann-nbc-settlement-covington-kid.

69 "Trump was right: 'Russian collusion' was a hoax. Good luck regaining public's trust.," Ingrid Jacques, USA TODAY, May 17, 2023, https://www.usatoday.com/story/opinion/columnist/2023/05/17/durham-report-vindicates-trump-fbi-russia-investigation/70222344007/

70 "25 Times Big Tech Claimed They Censored Conservatives by Mistake," Alexander Hall, Media Research Center, December 21, 2020, https://www.newsbusters.org/blogs/free-speech/alexander-hall/2020/12/21/25-times-big-tech-claimed-they-censored-conservatives

71 "Did Facebook just censor Jesus? Bizarre 'hate speech' message sparks concern," Billy Hallowell, *The Washington Times*, May 18, 2023, https://www.washingtontimes.com/news/2023/may/18/did-facebook-just-censor-jesus-bizarre-hate-speech/

72 "GOP senators push back against suggested 'no-fly list' for unruly passengers," Gregory Wallace and Pete Muntean, CNN, February 16, 2022, https://www.cnn.com/2022/02/16/politics/disruptive-passengers-faa-republicans/index.html

73 "State financial officers call on JPMorgan Chase to address politically motivated de-banking," Eric Revell, Fox Business, March 23, 2023, https://www.foxbusiness.com/politics/state-financial-officers-call-jpmorgan-chase-address-politically-motivated-de-banking

74 "Mozilla CEO Brendan Eich Resigns After Protests from Gay Marriage Supporters," ABC News, April 3, 2014, https://abcnews.go.com/Business/mozilla-ceo-resigns-calif-gay-marriage-ban-campaign/story?id=23181711

75 Arielle del Turco, "China to Christians: We're Rewriting the Bible, and You'll Use It or Else," *The Federalist*, October 26, 2020, https://thefederalist.com/2020/10/26/china-to-christians-were-rewriting-the-bible-and-youll-use-it-or-else/

76 Michael Burleigh, *Sacred Causes* (New York: Harper Publishing, 2007).

77 Scott Hahn and Benjamin Wiker, *Politicizing the Bible* (Chestnut Ridge, NY: Crossroad Publishing Company, 2013).

78 Richard Marsden, *The Soul of the American University* (Oxford, UK: Oxford University Press, 1994).

79 Murray Rothbard, *The Progressive Era* (Auburn, AL: Ludwig von Mises Institute, 2017).

80 Richard Gamble, *The War for Righteousness* (Wilmington, DE: ISI Books, 2004).

81 "The Presbyterian Minister's Son," *City Journal*, November 9, 2018, https://www.city-journal.org/article/the-presbyterian-ministers-son

82 Woodrow Wilson, *Congressional Government: A Study in American Politics* (1885); Woodrow Wilson, Constitutional Government in the United States (1908).

83 "When America's Most Prominent Socialist Was Jailed for Speaking Out Against World War I," Erick Trickey, Smithsonian, June 15, 2018, https://www.smithsonianmag.com/history/fiery-socialist-challenged-nations-role-wwi-180969386/

84 Edward J. Larson, "Prejudiced Results: Two Views of How Darwin Approached the Race Question," *BookForum*, February/March 2009, https://www.bookforum.com/print/1505/two-views-of-how-darwin-approached-the-race-question-3278.

85 Michael Flannery, "Darwin and Race: Three Strikes, He's Out," *Evolution News*, February 10, 2021. https://evolutionnews.org/2021/02/darwin-and-race-three-strikes-hes-out/

86 Charles Darwin to Charles Kingsley, University of Cambridge, Darwin Correspondence Project, February 6, 1862. https://www.darwinproject.ac.uk/letter/?docId=letters/DCP-LETT-3439.xml

87 Charles Darwin to William Graham, University of Cambridge, Darwin Correspondence Project, July 3, 1881. https://www.darwinproject.ac.uk/letter/?docId=letters/DCP-LETT-13230.xml

88 Ian Frazier, "When W. E. B. Du Bois Made a Laughingstock of a White Supremacist," *The New Yorker*, August 19, 2019, https://www.newyorker.com/magazine/2019/08/26/when-w-e-b-du-bois-made-a-laughingstock-of-a-white-supremacist

89 Ajitha Reddy, "The Eugenic Origins of IQ Testing: Implications for Post-Atkins Litigation," *De Paul Law Review*, Spring 2008, pp. 668-669, https://via.library.depaul.edu/cgi/viewcontent.cgi?article=1270&context=law-review

90 Daniel J. Flynn, Intellectual Morons: How Ideology Makes Smart People Fall for Stupid Ideas (New York: Crown Forum, 2004), 151.

91 Margaret Sanger, "America Needs a Code for Babies," *American Weekly*, March 27, 1934, Margaret Sanger Papers, Library of Congress, 128:0312B.

92 Flynn, *Intellectual Morons*, 152.

93 Robert G. Marshall and Charles A. Donovan, *Blessed Are the Barren: The Social Policy of Planned Parenthood* (San Francisco: Ignatius Press, San Francisco, 1991).

94 *Buck v. Bell*, 274 U.S. 200 (1927).

95 See https://www.plannedparenthood.org/about-us/who-we-are/our-history.

96 Writer/Director Mark Crutcher, *Maafa 21: Black Genocide* (video), 2009.

97 *The Liberator*, June 5, 1863, quoted in "Ballot Box, Jury Box, Cartridge Box," *Quote Investigator*, https://quoteinvestigator.com/2018/04/09/ballot/.

98 Robert Sherrill, *The Saturday Night Special* (New York: Charterhouse, 1973), 280–83, quoted in "Handguns," NRA Institute for Legislative Action, August 8, 2016, https://www.nraila.org/get-the-facts/handguns/.

99 Benjamin Wiker, "Science and the Natural Law," in *God's Grandeur: The Catholic Case for Intelligent Design*, (Manchester, N.H., Sophia Institute Press, 2023), Chapter 13.

100 Andrew Sullivan, "Is Intersectionality a Religion?" New York Magazine, March 10, 2017.http://nymag.com/daily/intelligencer/2017/03/is-intersectionality-a-religion.html.

101 Tunde Fatunde, "Scholars Focus on the Arab Trans-Saharan Slave Trade," *University World News*, April 13, 2012, https://www.universityworldnews.com/post.php?story=20120413180645205.

102 Sandeep Balakrishna, *Invaders and Infidels: From Sindh to Delhi, the 500-Year Journey of Islamic Invasions* (New Delhi: Bloomsbury, 2020).

103 Guenter Lewy, "Were American Indians the Victims of Genocide?" *Commentary*, September 2004, https://www.commentary.org/articles/guenter-lewy/were-american-indians-the-victims-of-genocide/.

104 Mark Stevenson, "Brutality of Aztecs, Mayas Corroborated," *Los Angeles Times*, January 23, 2005, https://www.latimes.com/archives/la-xpm-2005-jan-23-adfg-sacrifice23-story.html.

105 Julie McCarthy, "The Caste Formerly Known as 'Untouchables' Demands a New Role in India," NPR, August 13, 2016, npr.org/sections/goatsandsoda/2016/08/13/489883492/the-caste-formerly-known-as-untouchables-demands-a-new-role-in-india.

106 "Women who abort are at higher risk of many mental health problems. . . . The association between abortion and higher rates of anxiety, depression, substance use, traumatic symptoms, sleep disorders, and other negative outcomes is statistically significant in most analyses." David C. Reardon, "The Abortion and Mental Health Controversy: A Comprehensive Literature Review of Common Ground Agreements, Disagreements, Actionable Recommendations, and Research Opportunities," *SAGE Open Medicine* 6 (2018), https://www.ncbi.nlm.nih.gov/pmc/articles/PMC6207970/.

107 An organization called Negative Population Growth celebrates the fact that feminism leads to lower birthrates. See "New NPG Report: The Rise in Feminism and Its Impact on Population Growth: Birthrates and Female Empowerment Tied Together," Negative Population Growth, March 21, 2019, https://npg.org/wp-content/uploads/2019/09/03212019-PR-FP.pdf.

108 Robert Rector, "How Welfare Undermines Marriage and What to Do About It," Heritage Foundation, November 17, 2014, https://www.heritage.org/welfare/report/how-welfare-undermines-marriage-and-what-do-about-it.

109 "What Happens When Men Have Sex with Teenage Boys," Chad Felix Greene, Huffington Post, February 20, 2017, https://www.huffpost.com/entry/what-happens-when-men-have-sex-with-teenage-boys_b_58ab8c69e4b029c1d1f88e02

110 "Sex is a Biological Trait of Medical Significance," The American College of Pediatricians, March 2021, https://acpeds.org/position-statements/sex-is-a-biological-trait-of-medical-significance

111 "'Free Speech Is A Digital Black Plague': Bishop Garrison Is Key Mercenary in Biden's Dark War Against the First Amendment," *Revolver News*, May 12, 2021, https://www.revolver.news/2021/05/biden-race-mercenary-bishop-garrison-declares-war-first-amendment/.

112 Bishop Garrison, "The Modern Day Dark Age," *Inkstick*, July 26, 2018, https://archive.fo/c5btk.

113 Michael Graham, "Derryfield 'Inclusion' Group Demands School Remove Board Member Over Religious Beliefs," *NH Journal*, May 10, 2021, https://nhjournal.com/derryfield-inclusion-group-demands-school-remove-board-member-over-religious-beliefs/.

114 Private correspondence provided to the author by Ms. McGinley's legal counsel for use in reporting on her case.

115 Chelsey Cox, "Fact Check: Obama Administration Approved, Built Temporary Holding Enclosures at Southern Border," *USA Today*, August 26, 2020, https://www.usatoday.com/story/news/factcheck/2020/08/26/fact-check-obama-administration-built-migrant-cages-meme-true/3413683001/.

116 Victoria Bynum, James M. McPherson, James Oakes, Sean Wilentz, and Gordon S. Wood, "Re: The 1619 Project," *New York Times Magazine*, December 29, 2019, https://www.nytimes.com/2019/12/20/magazine/we-respond-to-the-historians-who-critiqued-the-1619-project.html.

117 Philip W. Magness, "Down the 1619 Project's Memory Hole," *Quillette*, September 19, 2020. https://quillette.com/2020/09/19/down-the-1619-projects-memory-hole/.

118 "The Protocols of the Elders of Zion," *The Holocaust Encyclopedia* (U.S. Holocaust Museum), https://encyclopedia.ushmm.org/content/en/article/protocols-of-the-elders-of-zion.

119 "The Protocols of the Elders of Zion."

120 Charles Kesler, "Call Them the 1619 Riots," *New York Post*, June 19, 2020, https://nypost.com/2020/06/19/call-them-the-1619-riots/.

121 See Allison Shuster, "Nikole Hannah-Jones Endorses Riots and Toppling Statues as a Product of the 1619 Project," *The Federalist*, June 20, 2020, https://thefederalist.com/2020/06/20/nikole-hannah-jones-endorses-riots-and-toppling-statues-as-a-product-of-the-1619-project/.

122 John Zmirak, "The Vatican's Alliance with China: More Evil Than We Thought," *The Stream*, January 13, 2020. https://stream.org/the-vaticans-alliance-with-china-more-evil-than-we-thought/.

123 Thomas Williams, "Whistleblower Claims Chinese Communists Pay Vatican $2 Billion in Bribes," *Breitbart*, June 23, 2020, https://www.breitbart.com/national-security/2020/06/23/whistleblower-claims-chinese-communists-pay-vatican-2-billion-in-bribes/.

124 Zak Doffman, "China Killing Prisoners to Harvest Organs for Transplant, Tribunal Finds," *Forbes*, June 8, 2019, https://www.forbes.com/sites/zakdoffman/2019/06/18/china-killing-prisoners-to-harvest-organs-for-transplant-tribunal-finds/#3af189a753d4.

125 Zhao Yusha, "Next Step for China, Vatican Is to Establish Diplomatic Ties, Top-Level Mutual Visits: Bishop," *Global Times*, December 9, 2019, https://web.archive.org/web/20210124041315/https://www.globaltimes.cn/content/1172791.shtml.

126 Harriet Sherwood, "Vatican Signs Historic Deal with China—but Critics Denounce Sellout," *The Guardian* (UK), January 30, 2018, https://www.theguardian.com/world/2018/sep/22/vatican-pope-francis-agreement-with-china-nominating-bishops.

127 Martin M. Barillas and Pete Baklinski, "'Intense' Spike in Christian Persecution After China's Secret Deal with Vatican: US Gov't Report," *LifeSite News*, January 9, 2020, https://www.lifesitenews.com/news/us-govt-report-vaticans-secret-deal-with-china-linked-to-intense-spike-in-catholic-persecution/.

128 According to the *Online Etymological Dictionary*, the word heresy originates from the "Greek hairesis 'a taking or choosing for oneself.'" Hence a heresy is a partial truth, substituted for the whole. https://www.etymonline.com/word/heresy

129 Anthony Sciglitano, *Marcion and Prometheus* (Chestnut Ridge, NY: Crossroad Publishing,: 2014).

130 John Zmirak, "The Seven Deadly Neuroses," *Aleteia*, June 12, 2013, https://aleteia.org/2013/06/12/the-seven-deadly-neuroses/.

131 Frédéric Bastiat, "That Which Is Seen, and That Which Is Not Seen," July 1815, http://bastiat.org/en/twisatwins.html#SECTION_G002.

132 George A. Akerlof and Janet L. Yellen, "An Analysis of Out-of-Wedlock Births in the United States," Brookings Institution, August 1, 1996, https://www.brookings.edu/research/an-analysis-of-out-of-wedlock-births-in-the-united-states/.

133 For historical statistics and a real-time body count, see the sobering website numberofabortions.com.

134 Jennifer A. Kingson, "Exclusive: $1 Billion-Plus Riot Damage Is Most Expensive in Insurance History," *Axios*, September 16, 2020, https://www.axios.com/riots-cost-property-damage-276c9bcc-a455-4067-b06a-66f9db4cea9c.html.

135 Jemima McEvoy, "14 Days of Protests, 19 Dead," *Forbes*, June 8, 2020, https://www.forbes.com/sites/jemimamcevoy/2020/06/08/14-days-of-protests-19-dead/?sh=139598d54de4; Ebony Bowden, "More Than 700 Officers Injured in George Floyd Protests Across US," *New York Post*, June 8, 2020, https://nypost.com/2020/06/08/more-than-700-officers-injured-in-george-floyd-protests-across-us/.

136 Jack Phillips, "Refunding the Police: Major Cities Backtrack on Police Budget Cuts After Crime Surges," *Epoch Times*, May 25, 2021, https://www.theepochtimes.com/mkt_breakingnews/refunding-the-police-major-cities-backtrack-on-police-budget-cuts-after-crime-surges_3830090.html.

137 "The Seattle Secessionists," *Wall Street Journal*, June 11, 2020, https://www.wsj.com/articles/the-seattle-secessionists-11591919047.

138 Rebecca Morin and Matthew Brown, "Kamala Harris Speech: January 6 Will 'Echo' in U.S. History Like Pearl Harbor, 9/11," USA Today, January 6, 2022, https://www.usatoday.com/story/news/politics/2022/01/06/harris-jan-6-like-pearl-harbor-9-11/9116617002/;Brian Bethune, "Was Jan. 6 the Beginning of the End for America?" *Maclean's*, January 4, 2022, https://macleans.ca/politics/washington/was-jan-6-the-beginning-of-the-end-for-america/; Dean Obeidallah, "George W. Bush Perfectly Tied 9/11 to the January 6 Attack," CNN, September 13, 2021, https://www.cnn.com/2021/09/12/opinions/bush-comments-9-11-terrorists-capitol-riot-obeidallah/index.html.

139 Julie Kelly, *January 6: How Democrats Used the Capitol Protest to Launch a War on Terror Against the Political Right*, New York, Bombardier Books, 2021.

140 Robert R. Reilly, *America on Trial* (San Francisco: Ignatius Press, 2020).

141 Jason Jones and John Zmirak, *The Race to Save Our Century* (Chestnut Ridge, NY: Crossroad Publishing Company, 2014).

142 Nels Erikson, *Nothing in Mitigation: Natural Law and the Nuremburg Trials*, (dissertation), University of North Dakota: 1984, https://commons.und.edu/theses/4392/

143 Martin Luther King Jr., "Letter from Birmingham Jail" (1963), https://billofrightsinstitute.org/activities/martin-luther-king-jr-letter-from-birmingham-jail-1963-pdj.

144 Matthew Arnold, "Dover Beach," https://www.poetryfoundation.org/poems/43588/dover-beach.

145 Rudyard Kipling, "Recessional" (1897), https://www.poetryfoundation.org/poems/46780/recessional.

146 Patrick Howley, "Obama Administration 'Placed Children With Human Traffickers,'" *Big League Politics*, May 29, 2018, https://bigleaguepolitics.com/obama-administration-placed-children-with-human-traffickers/.

147 Eduardo Verastegui, "Save Mexican and Central American Kids: Build the Wall," *The Stream*, May 15, 2019, https://stream.org/save-mexican-and-central-american-kids-build-the-wall/.

148 See Timothy P. Carney, "Honest Pro-Choicers Admit Roe v. Wade Was a Horrible Decision," Washington Examiner, January 22, 2011, https://www.washingtonexaminer.com/honest-pro-choicers-admit-roe-v-wade-was-a-horrible-decision.

149 *Planned Parenthood of Southeastern Pa. v. Casey* (91-744), 505 U.S. 833 (1992), https://www.law.cornell.edu/supct/html/91-744.ZO.html.

150 Jordan Boyd, "Here Are the Democrats Using the Leaked Dobbs Opinion as an Excuse to Demand Court-Packing," The Federalist, May 6, 2022, https://thefederalist.com/2022/05/06/here-are-the-democrats-using-the-leaked-dobbs-opinion-as-an-excuse-to-demand-court-packing/.

151 Maria Cramer and Jesus Jiménez, "Armed Man Traveled to Justice Kavanaugh's Home to Kill Him, Officials Say," New York Times, June 8, 2022, https://www.nytimes.com/2022/06/08/us/brett-kavanaugh-threat-arrest.html.

152 "Tracking Attacks on Pregnancy Centers & Pro-Life Groups," Catholic Vote (updated March 16, 2023), https://catholicvote.org/pregnancy-center-attack-tracker/.

153 Hadley Arkes, Josh Hammer, Matthew Peterson, and Garrett Snedeker, "A Better Originalism," The American Mind, March 18, 2021, https://americanmind.org/features/a-new-conservatism-must-emerge/a-better-originalism/?mc_cid=b864444b31.

154 "Arrival of the Fittest: Natural Selection as an Incantation," Evolution News, November 17, 2014, https://evolutionnews.org/2014/11/arrival_of_the/

155 Here are some good places to start:

(1) Stephen C. Meyer, *Return of the God Hypothesis* (New York: HarperOne, 2021). Meyer, a Cambridge-trained philosopher of science, explains, accessibly, the efforts of physicists like Stephen Hawking to evade the obvious implications of the Big Bang and explain away the fine-tuning of the universe for life via an imaginary "multiverse" for which we can never (in principle) find any evidence. You'll just have to take atheism on faith.

(2) Stephen C. Meyer, *Darwin's Doubt* (New York: HarperOne, 2013). This book shows how blind evolution cannot possibly account for the countless, complex mutations required to create the world's millions of species. Nor can random chance create entirely new "body plans" for the new genera of species that suddenly appeared in the Cambrian Explosion. Nor does the fossil record offer us clues, since it's missing most of the "missing links" Darwin predicted.

(3) Charles Thaxton et al., *The Mystery of Life's Origin* (Seattle: Discovery Institute, 2020). This multidisciplinary classic by eminent scientists has stood the test of decades. The new edition updates the classic with appendices by scientists working today. This scholarly book reveals that for decades, ever since scientists first tried creating life in a warm pond, there

has been zero progress in showing that "abiotic" chemistry could ever have spontaneously sparked life on earth.

(4) Matti Leisola and Jonathan Witt, *Heretic* (Seattle: Discovery Institute, 2018). Bioengineer Leisola gives a firsthand account of the personal and professional ruthlessness that scientists like him face if they raise any public doubts about Darwinist materialism. Such tactics don't prove Darwinism false, of course. But they do explain why a shaky theory can maintain the illusion of a consensus if its partisans are willing to use inquisitorial methods.

(5) Michael Behe, *Darwin Devolves* (New York: HarperOne, 2019). Bege, an eminent biologist, shows how genetic mutation seems never to build up the new, more elaborate DNA structures that neo-Darwinist theory requires to make possible ever higher, more developed forms of life. Instead, what few "evolutionary" developments we see from such mutations (that is, apparent improvements in fitness and hence survival) come from breaking existing genes, reducing the net information they contain. Try mutating from amoeba to activists that way.

(6) https://www.youtube.com/@DrJamesTour. Award-winning chemist and nanotechnology pioneer James Tour has produced hundreds of videos. In them, Dr. Tour rigorously subjects the entire origin-of-life field to scientific skepticism and explains in technical detail why most efforts to create even primitive organic mechanisms (amino acids, proteins, etc.) continue to fail—except when scientists rig them, acting as "intelligent designers" such as they claim never existed when life itself arose.

156 James Warren and Staff, "Sonny Steals the Show," *Chicago Tribune*, December 22, 1995, http://articles.chicagotribune.com/1995-12-22/features/9512220160_1_cher-rushmore-tv-guide.

157 Stephen C. Meyer, *The Signature in the Cell* (New York: HarperOne, 2009).

158 Thomas G. West, *The Political Theory of the American Founding* (Cambridge, UK: Cambridge University Press, , Cambridge, UK: 2017). A few more reading recommendations on Natural Law: J. Budziszewski, *What We Can't Not Know* (San Francisco: Ignatius Press, 2011); Edward Feser, *The Last Superstition* (South Bend, IN: St. Augustine's Press, 2010); Myron Magnet, *Clarence Thomas and the Lost Constitution* (New York: Encounter Books, 2019). The legal opinions of Justice Clarence Thomas offer a beacon of how Natural Law reasoning operates in the context of American jurisprudence.

159 Victoria Bynum, James M. McPherson, James Oakes, Sean Wilentz, and Gordon S. Wood, "Re: The 1619 Project," *New York Times Magazine*, December 29, 2019, https://www.nytimes.com/2019/12/20/magazine/we-respond-to-the-historians-who-critiqued-the-1619-project.html.

160 Jason Scott Jones, "Gun Rights: Human Rights Guaranteed by Natural Law," *Legatus*, April 1, 2016, https://legatus.org/news/gun-rights-human-rights-guaranteed-by-natural-law.

161 Brian Doherty, "How to Count the Defensive Use of Guns," *Reason*, March 9, 2015,https://reason.com/2015/03/09/how-to-count-the-defensive-use-of-guns//

162 Doherty, "How to Count the Defensive Use of Guns."

163 William English, PhD, "2021 National Firearms Survey," July 2021, https://papers.ssrn.com/sol3/papers.cfm?abstract_id=3887145.

164 Kimberly Holland, "What Are the 12 Leading Causes of Death in the United States?," *Healthline*, March 9, 2023. https://www.healthline.com/health/leading-causes-of-death#alzheimers-disease.

165 Richard V. Reeves and Sarah E. Holmes, "Guns and Race: The Different Worlds of Black and White Americans," Brookings Institution, December 15, 2015. https://www.brookings.edu/blog/social-mobility-memos/2015/12/15/guns-and-race-the-different-worlds-of-black-and-white-americans/.

166 Mark W, Smith, "Enlightenment Thinker Cesare Beccaria and His Influence on the Founders: Understanding the Meaning and Purpose of the Second Amendment's Right to Keep and Bear Arms," *Pepperdine Law Review* 71 (2020), https://digitalcommons.pepperdine.edu/cgi/viewcontent.cgi?article=2566&context=plr.

167 Eduardo Medina and Chris Cameron, "Missouri Governor Pardons St. Louis Couple Who Aimed Guns at Protesters," *New York Times*, August 3, 2021, https://www.nytimes.com/2021/08/03/us/politics/mark-patricia-mccloskey-pardon.html.

168 Richard M. Weaver, *Ideas Have Consequences* (Chicago: University of Chicago Press, 1948).

169 Jared Ball, "A Short History of Black Lives Matter," Real News Network, July 23, 2015 https://therealnews.com/pcullors0722blacklives.

170 Isabel Vincent, "Inside BLM Co-founder Patrisse Khan-Cullors' Million-Dollar Real Estate Buying Binge," New York Post, April 10, 2021, https://nypost.com/2021/04/10/inside-blm-co-founder-patrisse-khan-cullors-real-estate-buying-binge/.

171 Steve Sailer, "Black Homicide Deaths Went Up 53% During George Floyd Era," Unz Review, January 19, 2022, https://www.unz.com/isteve/black-homicide-deaths-went-up-53-during-george-floyd-era/

172 "Austria Orders Lockdown for Residents Who Have Not Received COVID-19 Vaccine," CBS News, November 15, 2021, https://www.cbsnews.com/news/austria-covid-lockdown-unvaccinated-residents/.

173 Alexandra Marshall, "Australia's White Elephant Zoo," *Spectator Australia*, October 12, 2022, https://www.spectator.com.au/2022/10/australias-white-elephant-zoo/.

174 David B. Kopel, *The Morality of Self-Defense and Military Action* (Santa Barbara, CA: Praeger Publishing, 2017).

175 Kopel, *The Morality of Self-Defense and Military Action*, 200.

176 "The Dechristianization of France during the French Revolution," Alberto M. Piedra, Institute of World Politics, January 12, 2018, https://www.iwp.edu/articles/2018/01/12/the-dechristianization-of-france-during-the-french-revolution/

177 "Aryanization," The Holocaust Encyclopedia, October 24, 2017, https://encyclopedia.ushmm.org/content/en/article/aryanization

178 Eric Metaxas, *Letter to the American Church* (Washington, DC: Salem Books, 2022).

179 Charles Norris Cochrane, *Christianity and Classical Culture* (Oxford: Oxford University Press, 1971). His account of the civic development of Rome and of Christian political philosophy undergirds the argument here throughout.

180 "Diocletian of Rome," Encyclopedia Brittanica, https://www.britannica.com/place/ancient-Rome/Barbarian-kingdoms

181 Peter Leithart, *Defending Constantine* (Westmont, IL: IVP Academic, 2010).

182 For a full account of the many innovations the clergy helped bring during the "Dark Ages," see Rodney Stark, *The Victory of Reason* (New York: Random House, 2007).

183 For fascinating stories of marginalized Christian groups that endured, see Philip Jenkins's *The Lost History of Christianity* (New York: HarperOne, 2008). Jenkins writes of the Donatists, who overemphasized Jesus's humanity compared to His divinity. Condemned by an ecumenical council, they continued to preach and practice, gravitating eastward toward Byzantium's fiercest rival, the Persian Empire. To spite Constantinople, the Persians welcomed Donatists, even as they persecuted orthodox Christian believers. Another group, the Monophysites, began as zealous enemies of the Donatists, and eventually they distorted Church doctrine to overemphasize . . . Jesus's divinity. They gained enormous popularity and influence in Egypt, whose Coptic church today is the heir of Monophysite clerics.

184 Historian Bat Ye'or documents this history in her comprehensive study *The Decline of Eastern Christianity Under Islam* (Madison, NJ: Fairleigh Dickinson University Press, 1996).

185 For the full story of the revolution Pope Gregory led, see Tom Holland, *Dominion* (New York: Basic Books, 2019).

186 Jonathan Riley-Smith, *The Crusades, Christianity, and Islam* (New York: Columbia University Press, 2011)

187 See Riley-Smith, and Rodney Stark, *God's Battalions* (New York: HarperOne, 2009).. Stark and Riley-Smith point out sources of the historical distortions. Anti-Catholic sentiment in the wake of the Reformation helped sour subsequent generations on the Crusades—especially after several popes wrongly declared "crusades" against Christian dissenters, such as the Hussites. Even worse, Enlightenment writers such as Voltaire falsely painted Muslim rulers as sophisticated and tolerant, and pretended that crusaders marched to enrich themselves and exterminate Muslims. Even the Romantic novelist Sir Walter Scott, otherwise a booster of things medieval, offered airbrushed portraits of Muslims as worldly and tolerant, while crusaders come off as avaricious bigots. See Ibn Warraq, *Sir Walter Scott's Crusades and Other Fantasies* (Nashville: New English Review Press, 2013).

188 Kopel, *The Morality of Self-Defense and Military Action*, 228.

189 Quoted in Kopel, 244.

190 Kopel, 272.

191 Kopel, 272.

192 Kopel, 274.

193 Kopel, 277.

194 Kopel, 277.

195 Kevin Phillips, *The Cousins' War* (New York: Basic Books, 1998).

196 Russell Kirk, *America's British Culture* (Piscataway, NJ: Transaction Publishers, 1993).

197 Kopel, *The Morality of Self-Defense and Military Action*, 297.

198 Samuel Gregg, *Tea Party Catholic* (Crossroad Publishing, Chestnut Hill, N.Y.: Crossroad Publishing, 2013).

199 Quoted in Kopel, *The Morality of Self-Defense and Military Action*, 297.

200 Joyce Lee Malcolm, *To Keep and Bear Arms* (Cambridge, MA: Harvard University Press, 1996).

201 Rebecca Beatrice Brooks, "What Was the Dominion of New England?," *History of Massachusetts Blog*, January 11, 2016, https://historyofmassachusetts.org/what-was-the-dominion-of-new-england/

202 "The Mayflower Compact: As an Idea, America Began in 1620, Not 1776," Lawrence Reed, *The Stream*, November 26, 2020, https://stream.org/the-mayflower-compact-as-an-idea-america-began-in-1620-not-1776/

203 David Hackett Fisher, *Albion's Seed* (New York: Oxford University Press, 1991).

204 Ellis Sandoz, ed., *Political Sermons of the American Founding Era* (Indianapolis, IN: Liberty Fund, 1998).

205 Patrick J. Deneen, *Why Liberalism Failed* (New Haven, CT: Yale University Press, 2019).

206 Reilly, *America on Trial*.

207 Joseph Loconte, *God, Locke, and Liberty* (Lanham, MD: Lexington Books, 2016).

208 John Locke, *A Letter Concerning Toleration and Other Writings* (Indianapolis, IN: Liberty Fund, 2010),https://oll.libertyfund.org/title/goldie-a-letter-concerning-toleration-and-other-writings .

209 Mark David Hall has painstakingly documented this hijacking in his indispensable book *Did America Have a Christian Founding?* (Nashville, TN: Thomas Nelson, 2019).

210 Mark W. Smith, *First They Came for the Gun Owners* (New York: Bombardier Books, 2019), Chapter 1.

211 Smith, Chapter 1.

212 Stephen P. Halbrook, *The Right to Bear Arms* (New York: Bombardier Books, 2021); Stephen P. Halbrook, *The Founders' Second Amendment* (Chicago: Ivan R. Dee, 2008).

213 *Federalist* No. 46 (James Madison), https://avalon.law.yale.edu/18th_century/fed46.asp.

214 "Battles of Lexington and Concord," History.com, January 14, 2020, https://www.history.com/topics/american-revolution/battles-of-lexington-and-concord.

215 Stephen P. Halbrook, *That Every Man Be Armed* (Albuquerque, NM: University of New Mexico Press, 2013), 7.

216 Joseph Story, *Commentaries on the Constitution* (1833), 3:§1890, https://press-pubs. uchicago.edu/founders/documents/amendIIs10.html.

217 For these examples and others, David B. Kopel, "Guns Kill People, and Tyrants with Gun Monopolies Kill the Most," *Gonzaga Journal of International Law* 24 (2021), https:// papers.ssrn.com/sol3/papers.cfm?abstract_id=3942071.

218 Kopel, "Guns Kill People, and Tyrants with Gun Monopolies Kill the Most." See also R. J. Rummel, *The Blue Book of Freedom* (Nashville, TN: Cumberland House, 2007).

219 See Kopel, "Guns Kill People, and Tyrants with Gun Monopolies Kill the Most"; David B. Kopel, Paul Gallant, and Joanne D. Eisen, "Is Resisting Genocide a Human Right?" *Notre Dame Law Review* 81, no. 4 (2006), https://scholarship.law.nd.edu/cgi/viewcontent. cgi?article=1347&context=ndlr.

220 Kopel, Gallant, and Eisen, "Is Resisting Genocide a Human Right?"

221 Rudyard Kipling, "The Gods of the Copybook Headings" (1919), https://www.kipling-society.co.uk/poem/poems_copybook.htm.

222 Read Mary Harrington's brilliant reflections on how hideous modern architecture and crackpot modernist thinking represented a spastic rejection of the generation that stumbled into combat in 1914: Mary Harrington, "What the Poppy Really Means," *Unherd*, November 11, 2021, https://unherd.com/2021/11/what-the-poppy-really-means/.

223 Ezra Pound, "Hugh Selwyn Mauberley (Part I)," https://www.poetryfoundation.org/ poems/44915/hugh-selwyn-mauberley-part-i.

224 See numberofabortions.com.

225 Ida B. Wells-Barnett, *Southern Horrors: Lynch Law in All Its Phases* (1892), https://www. gutenberg.org/files/14975/14975-h/14975-h.htm.

226 Yuliya Parshina-Kottas, Anjali Singhvi, Audra D. S. Burch, Troy Griggs, Mika Gröndahl, Lingdong Huang, Tim Wallace, Jeremy White, and Josh Williams, "What the Tulsa Race Massacre Destroyed," *New York Times*, May 24, 2021, https://www.nytimes.com/ interactive/2021/05/24/us/tulsa-race-massacre.html; Ben Fenwick, "The Massacre That Destroyed Tulsa's 'Black Wall Street,'" *New York Times*, July 13, 2020, https://www.nytimes. com/2020/07/13/us/tulsa-massacre-graves-excavation.html.

227 "Tracking Attacks on Pregnancy Centers & Pro-Life Groups," Catholic Vote (updated March 16, 2023), https://catholicvote.org/pregnancy-center-attack-tracker/.

228 Kim Roberts, "Firebombed Pregnancy Center Conducts Private Investigation into Violence," *Religion Unplugged*, January 19, 2023, https://religionunplugged.com/ news/2023/1/12/firebombed-pregnancy-center-conducts-private-investigation-into-violence.

229 Helen Raleigh, "U.S. Navy Pushes Transgender Pronouns While Allowing Massive War-Preparedness Gaps," *The Federalist*, June 24, 2022, https://thefederalist.com/2022/06/24/u-s-navy-pushes-transgender-pronouns-while-allowing-massive-war-preparedness-gaps/.

230 "2019 Report on International Religious Freedom: Iraq," U.S. Department of State, Office of International Religious Freedom, https://www.state.gov/reports/2019-report-on-international-religious-freedom/iraq/

231 "A Timeline of Disaster and Displacement for Iraqi Christians."

232 "Like Britain in 1940, Syria's Kurds and Christians Stand Alone," Johannes de Jong, The Stream, February 8, 2018, https://stream.org/like-britain-1940-syrias-kurds-christians-stand-alone/

233 Thomas Schmidinger, *The Autonomous Administration of North and East Syria: Between a Rock and a Hard Place* (London: Transnational Press, 2020).